My
Being
With
Beings

Leon J Morris

Contents

This book is dedicated to my wife and son without whose love and support I would not be here today to witness this creation with Spirit become manifest. And for that I am truly grateful.

Acknowledgements

Firstly to all the beautiful beings of love and light who so generously blended their energies with mine and shared their knowledge, wisdom and guidance through me to manifest this book into being, thank you.

To our dear friend Ann Tattam, both Julia and I are so grateful to you for bringing my vague descriptions and sketches to life in a far more wonderful way that we could've hoped for. Thank you Ann.

And to my beautiful twin flame Julia, for your help in ensuring this book got finished not just giving me much needed feedback and advice but, more importantly, by always making sure I had the time and space to focus on getting it done, for motivating me to stay on track and, above all else, for filling up my love tank when I had been running on empty for so long. Thank you my darling, darling.

Introduction

As with all journeys it is best to start somewhere, anywhere, as long as you start, and go from there.

So, this is my somewhere and we'll see where it takes us.

Firstly, I'd like to say that this book is not meant to be about me or my life story. I only intend to give you a picture of how and why I have come to this point in my life where I have chosen to share this experience; this magical part of my journey with you.

In each meditation you will notice the use of italics. This is to signify when it is Spirit speaking to me or relaying a message. The normal text is me speaking or asking Spirit a question.

In Chapter Six when I recount my past lives and at the end of Chapter Seven with my final thought, there are no italics as it is only me sharing an experience or my thoughts.

When I mention "Source Energy" I am referring to the energy you might commonly think of as God, or whichever name you use depending on your religious affinities or beliefs. When I talk about "Spirit" I am referring to Ascended Masters, Angels, Spirit Guides and other etheric beings.

Finally, when I talk about "physical beings" I mean those beings who exist in physical Realms; either our own or the others in existence. In simple terms I mean what you would think of as "aliens".

I hope this makes clear what is going on as you move through the book.

Whoever you are, wherever you are and on whatever stage of your journey you are, I share what is within as a fellow spiritual being having a human experience; desiring to fulfil my purpose in this life. Therefore I offer to you the information which has been lovingly shared with me.

What you do with this information, if anything, is entirely up to you. As with everything in life, it is always your choice. I would simply ask you to go in with an open mind and an open heart in the hope there may come a moment when something stirs in you and releases a spark of light to illuminate that which has been hidden in the shadows of your mind; the beautiful truth of who you are and the purpose of your own journey.

Once you discover your purpose in this life you may consider yourself truly fortunate for no soul comes to understand, or even know, their purpose in a single lifetime.

It can take many lives to finally become aware of what you are here to accomplish.

My epiphany, after the many lives I have so far discovered, only came to me in my current life; during my early forties.

I'd been watching YouTube videos of a woman who, through her hypnotherapy practice, came to realise that she needed to share all the information which Spirit shared through her sessions with clients.

As I was watching her, something just clicked inside me and I knew beyond doubt that my purpose in this life is to share as she did, to share as others who have come before did and as others who come after will do.

I very nearly didn't live to have this epiphany and would have had to start all over again in yet another lifetime. This was because of an unexpected illness in 2015. My condition suddenly deteriorated on the day I was due to be discharged from hospital, to the point that the surgeon matter-of-factly told me, "Leon, if we do not operate now, you will be dead in 3-4 hours."

As daunting as it was for Julia and me to hear those words, I was not afraid as I truly didn't believe I would die that day. All I can tell you is I had a sense of knowing; a comforting feeling deep inside that told me, as traumatic and painful as it would be to endure, it was not the end of this particular journey. There was still more to be done. A purpose to discover, to be fulfilled and further evolution to be achieved.

Evidently I did survive and here I am, focused on fulfilling my true purpose at last. So, with my purpose in mind, I invite you to allow me to begin sharing with you.

CHAPTER ONE

My spiritual journey so far.

Journeys are made up of moments. It is what you do in those moments that counts.

The focus of the moments on this particular journey are all spiritual at their core, and I feel relevant here. My life so far has been filled with a vast array of experiences. It has been full of wonderful highs and difficult lows; some incredibly life changing and path changing moments which brought me to this moment right now, sat here diligently trying to write this book.

The first spiritual experience I remember goes back to around the age of eleven or twelve. I was living in East London at the time. Our end-of-terrace house was on the same road as the last of the many primary schools I'd attended, due to moving with or between parents.

This road, as with many others, had been bombed during the Second World War, and there had apparently been fatalities. My primary school was rumoured to be haunted. I still don't know whether or not that was true, but the building itself was definitely creepy enough in the minds of young children to cause such a rumour to be created.

There were the inevitable dares to go up to the top floor and try to see the ghost in the attic, but as much as we acted brave, none of us ever did go up there and find out for sure.

I'm digressing, as I often do, but this will take on relevance shortly. Anyway, back to the first experience we go. I don't remember the exact day, time or date, as I am writing this some 30 years after the event took place, but I will always remember the experience.

It is late night heading into the early hours of the morning.

The ever-present lights of London create the soft orange glow which fills my room. I'm fast asleep but I am becoming aware of a feeling; a knowing that I am somewhere between the dream state and being awake.

I feel as though my body has become lighter. It's strange but not scary. In fact the feeling is simply peaceful.

Then, even though my eyes are closed, I can see myself floating above myself.

Suddenly I'm standing by my bed, dispassionately observing my motionless body lying there sound asleep. I don't know how long this lasted but I do know that, in that moment, I felt like I had a choice to make.

I could choose to leave my body for good or return to it and continue this journey, accepting all that would follow.

I made my choice.

Now here I am; writing, working, laughing, crying, smiling, shouting, loving, breathing, living and experiencing all that this life has brought, and has yet to bring me.

The following morning, I woke up feeling a little stunned by the experience, yet I had a welcome calmness and peace that was unusual for me during those years of my life.

This calm peacefulness stayed with me for some days and I was incredibly grateful for it.

The next experience I want to share is a combination of things that happened during my early teens in that same house.

I was fourteen or fifteen and for a period of time I would hear a scratching noise in the dining and living room ceiling.

I mentioned it to my Mum and her boyfriend at the time but I was the only one who ever heard it. Their first thought was that it must be a rat, we lived in London so that was an understandably rational explanation. They laid rat poison in the cellar and we waited, checked, waited and checked.

We never did trap the rat, nor did we find any evidence of rodents being in our house at all.

The noise continued and I was still the only one who could hear it. I stopped talking about the scratching as it became yet another thing that would often annoy my mum and her boyfriend.

If I'm really honest, I began to get a bit freaked out by it myself.

During this time I had moved into the loft which had been converted into an extra bedroom. Being a teenager I was extremely happy about this. After all, what teenager doesn't want their own space?

I had moved my precious essentials up there with me including my beloved games console; the incredible zx spectrum which was a must have of the eighties (at least in my opinion) and my hi-fi unit on which my best friend and I would play our vinyl records. I also had a tape recorder next to my bed which I would sometimes use to record my thoughts on blank tapes or play my favourite albums.

An annoying feature of this tape recorder was that when you adjusted the volume dial it would make a loud crackling noise, which isn't ideal when it's late at night and you're supposed to be asleep, but are instead trying to quietly play music until tiredness finally takes over.

One afternoon I was home alone. I'd finished all my chores for the morning, so decided to head upstairs and listen to some music.

As I'm climbing up the ladder into my room, I hear static, like white noise coming out of my stereo speakers which are above me to my left. I was sure I had turned it off earlier and didn't think much of it until I looked down and saw that it was completely unplugged.

I froze on the ladder, either in fear or shock I'm not sure.

As the realisation that something "different" is going on begins to dawn on me, I hear my tape recorder volume, several feet away from me, start loudly crackling away.

Bear in mind that this was only possible if you physically moved the volume dial with your finger and I'm currently frozen on the ladder with only my head in the room.

Needless to say I was completely freaked out and proceeded to get downstairs faster than a greyhound out of the traps, chasing a fake rabbit around Walthamstow dog track!

I remember thinking; it's not the school being haunted I should've been worried about, it's my house.Not long after this, there was one more incident which took place there.

The downstairs layout of the living area as you entered from the front door was a corridor which led in to an open plan living/dining room, then onto the kitchen which in turn led to the conservatory and a tiny concrete paved garden. Again I was home alone and sat in the kitchen. I finished eating my lunch and decided to go watch a video on the VHS recorder in the living room.

As I'm walking through the dining room, I begin to hear scratching in the ceiling again.

I stop suddenly.

Standing there frozen I feel drawn to look through the archway toward the right side of the living room.

My eyes move over to the framed mirror with the alcoholic beverage print which is hanging on the wall.

This mirror proceeds to lift itself off the picture hook, come about an inch or so away from the wall, hang in mid air for the briefest moment, then drop onto the radiator and crack apart.

Now, I don't really know anything about physics but I'm pretty sure framed mirrors aren't supposed to be able to lift themselves off wall hooks, levitate, then drop onto the radiator all by themselves.

Obviously I was a bit unsettled by these events, which I got the blame for, because who in their right mind would believe anyone who told them what I had just witnessed.

It all stopped after that.

Although it seemed a bit unnerving to me at first, knowing what I know now has removed any fear of such occurrences.

It wasn't a "haunting" it was simply Spirits' way or a spirits way of trying to get my attention because they knew something I hadn't come to realise as yet.

I was and always have been psychic.

I just didn't understand it for many years, well not to the degree I do now anyway.

Skipping forward eight years, I was dating a girl who after a few months confided in me that her mum was Clairvoyant and her dad also had a strong psychic ability.

I was outside her parents house with her dad one evening. We were having a chat about their psychic abilities during which he told me that I was also very psychic but wouldn't realise it, or be able to use this ability until I was close to forty years old.

We finished our conversation, went inside and I gave it no more thought. To be honest I wasn't at all religious or even spiritual back then, although I'd flirted with the idea of religion having been to a baptist church and bible study group for a year of my teens.

I went through my twenties with a completely non spiritual mindset shall we say, without going into details. At the end of my twenties I went off backpacking around the world, what an incredible life changing experience that was. If you've done it yourself then you will certainly know what I mean.

When I came back I decided to return to church for another go at the religion thing. I even became a born again Christian. However, I came to realise, for various reasons, that organised religion really just isn't for me and never went back.

Throughout my life I have always had "questions" and have been seeking not only answers, but something else I couldn't describe for many years.

A knowing deep inside myself of a purpose I needed to accomplish with this life I'd chosen to stay in before it was all over.

Jumping forward again I'm now thirty-eight. Out of the blue I make contact with an old school friend who I haven't seen for twenty-one years. We spend the next few months developing a relationship online and eventually, after much pursuing, Julia allows me to visit her in North Cyprus where she's currently living.

She is a very spiritual woman and it is during a Skype call one evening that I get the first chance to see this side of her. I don't remember exactly what we were talking about at the time, most probably a mix of small talk and flirting knowing us, but as I'm talking to her I notice she has become a little distracted.

Suddenly she says, "You sleep on the left side of your bed, don't you."

I said yes, how do you know that?

She replies, "Oh because I can see that when your Grandad, from your mothers side, is with you he sits on the right side of your bed at night, watching over you."

My initial response was essentially, erm, what now? Especially as my mums' dad died when I was still a toddler. I was stunned into silence yet also quite intrigued by this new aspect of her.

As time went by I began to get used to Julia's ability to know things she couldn't possibly know. During my holiday to North Cyprus that she would give me further insight into this spiritual side of her.

It is a balmy summers' afternoon. As we lay outside on the balcony looking up at the clear blue sky, she asks me if I want to learn how to see energy and auras.

I am still not a believer but have become more open minded with age, so I decide to go along with it and see what happens.

With a very simple technique, she shows me how. I'm not sure what I'm looking for exactly but then I begin to see it.

An invisible line between our index fingers suddenly becomes visible. Like it was out of focus until I was able to tune into the correct frequency for it to become clear. I see energy everywhere now, all around me and I am completely blown away by one of the most magical moments I have ever experienced.

Throughout the following years it became clear to us that we have a deeply profound connection, one that has been shared over many lifetimes. There is also a divine purpose to our coming into each others awareness once more. A purpose which is being continuously revealed in such a beautiful and magical way.

Six weeks after returning to England, I moved to North Cyprus for the foreseeable future and began to read spiritual books and magazines, watch related videos online, wear crystal pendants, bracelets, the works. I'm fully signed up now, hungry for more, give me the t-shirt too mate!

Five months into this new chapter of my life I went to visit a medium with over thirty years experience in spiritual work. At the end of my reading she tells me I apparently have a psychic ability and decides to invite me to come along to the "psychic circle" she leads every fortnight to develop it.

After she kindly explains what a psychic circle actually is, I gratefully accept her invitation.

Driving back I can't wait to get home and explain it all to Julia. I get to the apartment, walk through the door with a huge smile on my face and I see Julia is there waiting for me, excited to find out how it went.

As I'm explaining it all to her something dawns on me.

The following year I will turn forty, in an instant I'm drawn back to the conversation I had as a twenty-two year old with my ex-girlfriend's dad.

I am briefly lost for words as the realisation of his prediction hits me like a ton of bricks. In that moment I feel a mixture of excitement and wonder at the possibilities of the experiences which lay ahead during this next stage of my life.

Three months into my attendance at the psychic circle, Julia was invited to join us as well. To be able to share this with her and see her develop as a medium was a blessing.

Although we only attended this circle for just over two years, I can honestly say that the wonderful experiences we had during that time are too numerous to mention here.

My development as a medium was quite quick and I was told that, along with many others around the world, I was being "fast tracked" to be able to fulfill my purpose.

I went from being very nervous, feeling quite intimidated and thinking; I'm in a room full of mediums, who am I trying to kid? I'm not going to get anything, I can't do this. To becoming a trance medium who channels various beings from various dimensions.

I will always be grateful to the people of that circle, as well as the generous souls who stepped forward to allow us to practice our mediumship abilities with them.

Thank you.

I have been privileged to channel amazing beings who lovingly share wisdom, give guidance and bring much needed light into this world.

At first I was a bit unnerved by the experience but with encouragement from those people around me, I relaxed and learned to flow with it.

To let go of resistance to it, to not try so hard once I was comfortable with it and now I am at peace with it, incredibly grateful for the ability and for the opportunity to be able to have this experience.

Learning to meditate and all the experiences that have come with it has changed me in many ways, to the point that those who know me best, see a huge difference in me.

Such as being visibly happier, relaxed and more at ease within myself and with life in general.

The anger, moodiness and low self worth that were all too prevalent in me had been replaced with love, happiness and a new sense of self worth, as well as the realisation that I do actually deserve all the good stuff.

For many years, during and after my childhood, I was so angry and bitter that an intense dark rage would often engulf and consume me to the point that I would want to harm whoever I felt had wronged me. Other times I would be deeply depressed and have serious suicidal thoughts on a regular basis. I would plan exactly how, when and where I would do it.

When I was fifteen I went a step further and made an attempt to hang myself.

I had got to a point of such despair, desperation almost, due to the bullying at home and at school, the mental and physical abuse, as well as the overwhelming feeling of complete and utter loneliness.

Over the course of many years I had been systematically stripped of any individuality, through the total control of every action and emotion I was allowed to have, often being told with a quietly threatening and sinister tone of voice; How to be, how to stand, how to walk, what level of gratitude was to be shown when receiving gifts, how I should say thank you, and exactly how to smile.

All the while knowing I would be watched closely

to see if I'd performed as desired, the constant threat of punishment hanging over me for even the littlest things, the severity of which would vary greatly if I didn't carry out their instructions to a satisfactory level. I allowed my fear of them to completely control me.

The never knowing when it was coming or what for or how severe it would be was difficult to deal with. I found myself feeling like I was constantly walking on eggshells, trying to find ever more creative ways not to set them off.

One afternoon after I returned home from school, the house was empty and I decided today was the day.

I sought out an old leather belt of mine with a studded horse shoe buckle which had been previously used for a different purpose, not just to hold up my jeans.

After being taken to a grass running track for our P.E lesson by the school, the bus was delayed and we were late getting back. In my panic I threw my clothes on over my P.E kit and ran home as fast as I could.

As I walked through the door I was asked where I had been and why I was late. I explained in fine detail everything that happened and said sorry several times. My explanation and apology were accepted, I'd got away with it.

As I sat on the sofa to watch tv, I was suddenly asked; "What's that under your clothes?" I didn't know what had been seen at first but then it hit me and my heart sank. I would not be getting away with anything today.

I was then made to take off my top layer of clothes, leaving me in the offending kit, and lay face down on the living room floor while I was angrily beaten with the belt and buckle as my mothers boyfriend sat in the arm chair watching, either the tv or me I'm not sure. I was ten years old.

As much as this was my punishment for wearing

my P.E kit under my clothes when I had been told once before that it was not allowed, there was also the added aspect of my lateness that caused the increase in severity.

My PE kit happened to be my beloved Liverpool football kit which my Nanny, my dad's mum, had bought for me as a gift.

To add insult to injury, and I felt out of sheer spite, I was told to take it off and that it would be cut up then thrown in the bin as previously promised. I pleaded with her not too but I could see it was making her angry again so thought better of it.

When I came back downstairs, I asked where my kit was? In reply she proudly pointed to the kitchen bin and said, "There."

I was guilty as charged, on both counts, but I hadn't done it out of defiance. It had been the fear of getting home late, because if I was literally sixty, thirty or even twenty-seconds late at any time, I would be in trouble and there would be a consequence of some sort.

There was more to my childhood than this and these are only some examples of what I experienced, but as I said before this book is not meant to be about my life story so there's no need to go into too much detail here.

I didn't particularly want to write much about this period of my life at all but felt it necessary to give a better understanding of how I had gotten to such a low point, and why I carried around such negative emotions for so long.

I know there are people out there who have had to deal with far worse than I did but, with me being a very sensitive child, I took it to heart much more than maybe some would.

I had reached out to some family members. I told them what had been happening to me, but it got me nowhere, so it continued and I spiralled deeper into my misery.

So I chose that particular belt for the significance

of its use back then, and the subsequent impact I hoped it would have on them.

Stood there on the extendable ladder as I tied it around the bannister of the entrance to my attic bedroom, I thought about the looks on their faces. I thought about how they would try to cover it up, the denial, the deflection of blame to anyone or anything else apart from them. No matter what they said or did they wouldn't be able to keep up false pretences anymore, not after this.

No more secrets behind closed doors. The truth would have to be acknowledged. This would be my revenge for all the hurt they had caused.

As much as I wanted all of the above and to end what I considered my miserable excuse of a life, I was still afraid, which made me angry enough to attempt to go through with it.

But as I tentatively stepped off the ladder, feeling the belt slowly tighten around my neck, I became aware of a voice deep within me, urging me not to go out this way, battling with myself, with all the anger, desire for revenge, misery, loneliness and self loathing to somehow find the strength to continue being.

I stepped back onto the ladder, removed the belt and cried briefly before telling myself that people were right; I am weak, I am pathetic, I couldn't even be brave enough or tough enough to go through with it.

I hated myself and my life because I believed all the negative things that were said to me growing up. I was so focused on so many negative aspects of my existence that I became exactly who I didn't want to be, who they told me I was.

I wished I'd chosen to leave rather than stay during my out of body experience as a child.

I hated these people for how much they made me hate myself and my life. I laid the blame for this firmly at the door of those who had hurt me the most, due to their actions and words which I had allowed to affect me so profoundly.

It was at this point I went along to the Baptist church for that year of my teens.

Reflecting back on those experiences now I have come to realise something. All the things that happened to me, and because of me, helped to bring me to this point, to my current perspective, via many valuable lessons.

Lessons which showed me what I don't want and who I don't want to be, which in turn taught me to better understand what I do want and who I do want to be.

As hard as it was to go through some of those experiences, I know I wouldn't have survived till now if I hadn't had them and for that I am truly grateful.

I'd like to end this chapter with some advice that was lovingly given and received in meditation on Thursday 6th December 2018.

You are caught in a silent trap within your mind. You believe what you see and in turn see what you believe to be reality. But this is only your perspective of what is real based on that which you have been conditioned to believe.

"What is truth? What is real reality? Am I here? Or is here, there? I am confused because everything is confusing".

You are a spiritual being, an energy force, existing in a physical reality which has been constructed for your experience so that you, and we, may achieve greater knowing, which in turn causes us to further evolve and draw ever closer to returning to Source.

All that we experience, all that exists and occurs, is for the ultimate purpose of this journey.

So, with everything that you experience, ask yourself this; What can I learn from this lesson so that I may evolve and draw ever closer to Source? Then open yourself to receiving the wisdom and guidance which is waiting for you, to help you to achieve this goal.

You have been told to "do unto others as you would have them do unto you". We would say, share knowledge as it has

knowingly been shared with you. And if you must know why?
For love.

This is your purpose. This is what you do next.

How you do this is up to you, there are many forms to
choose from so that you may achieve this common goal.

CHAPTER TWO

Questions

I, like all of us, have had and will have many questions that we would love definitive answers to.

During one particular meditation, I was given several questions by Spirit which they suggested I ask individually at another time. When I did I found many different beings stepped forward to answer these questions.

As a medium it is up to me to interpret the information I receive as accurately as I can, into what is essentially a crude and primitive system of communication. I'm talking about the English language.

I honestly don't mean that in a derogatory sense, it's simply a case of spoken language not being necessary for the spirit realms or with advanced beings of various dimensions. The best way I can describe it is this, communication is done much more effectively and efficiently through thoughts, feelings and the instantaneous knowing of both.

I trust the interpretation I offer here is what Spirit intended to be shared.

What exactly happens when we die?

Imagine if you will a trance-like state as if you're between the waking and the sleeping world or realm.

This is where it begins.

You are first joined by your guide or guides as their energy feels familiar to you. This is comforting, as remembering can be quite jolting for your soul energy. They will help ease the transition from physical to spiritual awareness.

Once you are deemed ready and you are at peace with what is happening, with where you are, you will be joined by your Guardian Angel. They will symbolically hold your hand and assist you to feel the energy of spirit at gradually increasing levels.

You will see and feel a cacophony of coloured light, this is your true self adjusting to its new environment once more. There is no definition or measurement of time here for this process. It simply occurs until your transition is complete.

The next step is connecting with members of your soul group who are currently in spirit, this helps to ground you in this realm. Everything is done in stages, with love and gentleness. All is gentle and peaceful here.

It is truly a time for rejoicing and respite for your soul after the trauma of physical life and death. Your vibration will continue to rise and as it does so you will connect with more beings in this realm.

Once your vibration has reached a certain point, you will be able to visit the physical realm briefly to comfort those beings who you left behind. This is done with love for those who remain as they are not able to see and experience, the truth and beauty of who we are and where we exist after we are released from the constraints of the physical realm.

Your soul is energy, pure energy. It can take multiple forms and reside in innumerable hosts. In the spirit realm, you are free to go where you please at the speed of thought. Should you desire to go somewhere that is unknown to you, then help will be given to take you there so long as it is permitted. You may only experience realms that your soul energy has evolved to cope with, there are more places that just are not possible for you yet, at least not those of you who exist in this universe.

Because you have been released from the physical body, and realm, you will vibrate at a faster rate as your higher self, so communicating with your guides and Guardian Angel will be easier and clearer. Therefore it will also be easier for you to attain a greater rate of evolution and flow toward the next stage of experience.

You will continue to be guided, you will be permitted to visit such places as the great hall of knowledge. This place is a reality for all those of you who require it at various stages of evolution. Only the areas that contain the truths you can comprehend will be available to you until you no longer have a need for them.

The great halls can take the form of a vast library, it would take up many acres of land on Earth. Huge pillars, marble floors, wooden doors, or not. It will take the form that feels acceptable to your perspective.

Here you will be led through your physical life on earth to understand each experience, its purpose for you and how you can use it to evolve further. You can and sometimes do repeat experiences from previous lives to either facilitate your own or another soul's evolution.

Continuation of the same question in a separate meditation;

Continuing on from where we left off, once you have visited with your loved ones you return to the spirit realm, not that you actually left, but that's another question for another time. Your re-emergence continues in the "waiting area" if you like.

You are left to absorb the contents of the life you have just lived, you will find yourself looking at the contents from a less emotional, attached perspective of one who is living the life, rather it is with a more detached, balanced, observational higher perspective of all the events experienced.

As you become in tune with your true self, you may decide, upon review, that you have experienced or learned everything that you needed to from that life. Or you may desire to experience some aspects again, either from a different perspective or because there was a "lesson left unlearned".

This process of reincarnation can occur as long as you desire it. If you are content then you move to the next stage; Reintegration.

Reintegration into the spiritual realms is a gentle process which you are guided through. You will be enabled to raise your vibration to a sufficient level so that you may exist here. Your guide or guides will be with you throughout.

Here you exist more as an energetic vibration of your consciousness rather than physical matter. You are able to think, know and comprehend more, but feel less. You do not have a need for the five human senses, or the sixth, as you no longer need to tune into Spirit, consciousness, your higher self, whatever you wish to term it.

Now you are Spirit, you are consciousness and your higher self existing at a higher level of vibration. You continue to tune in, expand, and reintegrate until you are ready for the next stage; Remembrance.

Here we reach the limits of human understanding or what your mind at its current vibrational rate can comprehend. Remembrance takes place in another realm of existence that vibrates on yet a higher level or at a faster rate.

There is not a great deal that we can tell you about this place, as it is something which can only be experienced and not foretold. Simply know that it is there, it is beautiful beyond words, and that you will experience it.

Death in the sense that you are born, you live, you pay taxes and you die, then there is nothing, or worse, a heaven and hell to consider, just simply is not true.

Death in this sense is a low vibrational concept brought about to install fear and assume greater control over the mind of a soul.

It is not done in a sinister way by evil, unseen people or foes. It is only an aspect of the experience we chose to have when we incarnate into the physical realm.

However, the moment has come to remove this aspect, as it no longer serves us or you. It is now necessary for beings to remove the fear of death so that a faster rate of evolution may begin.

Therefore we say this to you; Know that all souls live on forever, and by forever we mean all eternity. There is no, nor has there ever been true death of any soul in existence.

Truly we ask you to know beyond knowing, to accept in the deepest levels of your consciousness, that you are eternal.

This is truth beyond measure.

Remove, if you will, any fear of death as you think of it, right now in this very moment. For death does not exist in any realm, yet you do and you will forever.

Life

Who created Humans? How did we come to be?

You were created by a thought. A conscious desire to bring you into existence. You came to be in an instant, as soon as the thought occurred you were created.

Evolution as you know it, in your instance at least, did occur. You started as cells in the oceans, but it was always known that you would become sentient beings.

Think of it like you performed a science experiment of new and wondrous discovery but you created the conditions knowing exactly what the outcome would be. The outcome is who you are today, as in sentient physical beings.

The next step in your evolution will be to become a lot closer to your spiritual selves whilst still existing in a physical realm. As a result, your understanding of the universe, of the laws of science, of technology and nature will move forward in leaps and bounds.

You will travel through space, you will make contact with other sentient beings existing in the physical realms, that's not to say they haven't made contact with you, it is more that you have not reached a vibrational frequency as a whole where you can access communication with them, or where they want you to be as a people before allowing general contact and interaction to occur.

Open contact will be made within the 21st century, progress will be made in the 22nd century of your physical time.

Going back to the first question, it is not "who" but rather what created you.

Life created you, the life force of the Source Energy.

This consciousness that exists in a way you absolutely cannot yet comprehend, had the thought which brought forth the process, which would set in motion another aspect of creation.

This thought occurred with the greatest love you could possibly imagine, a love beyond love. Imagine parents love, especially a mothers love for her child, magnified exponentially, infinitely. That is close to the state of love in which this thought took place.

No scientist or religion can explain the truth of what this being is. It is something which can only be known to the most evolved souls who are closest to rejoining with the Source of all things.

It cannot be expressed in words, it can only be known.

There will come a state of being in which you comprehend, in which you know the truth of this, but not yet.

So, for now you must continue on your path of evolutionary experience, understanding and knowing until you reach a place of such peace and bliss that you will once more be at one with yourself and all that is. Remember, love is.

How do we gain deeper understanding of what is?

There is no hierarchy as such. In other realms, it is more like multiple levels of awareness, innumerable vibrational frequencies that exist to assist each other in achieving their purpose.

To evolve and eventually rejoin the Source Energy from which they came.

In your current vibrational frequency, you are simply not able to comprehend the truth of this, at some stage you will, but only when you reach another state of being.

Know now, every idea you have regarding the laws of physics or the religious doctrines you follow, and hold so dear, are only true to you because of your current vibrational frequency.

It is not true for those of us existing in different realms with greater, or should I say a clearer, awareness of what is. That which is, is truth, light and above all, love.

The more you open yourself to connecting with beings of higher or more evolved vibrational frequencies, the more you evolve, and will attune your frequency more clearly with ours.

In turn, your capacity for understanding, for knowing that which is, increases dramatically.

There is so much for you to learn, this is not a derogatory statement, but rather an indication of the excitement we hold to see your journey unfold as ours once did.

All of you who exist in the physical realm of earth are at an incredibly important juncture in your existence, which is known as "the great awakening". This has happened before, when you first became aware that you are conscious beings, and it will happen again throughout your groups' evolution.

As we said this is called the great awakening and it is the second phase of your evolution.

This is when you become more open as a whole to the idea that you are truly more than just physical beings. You will be privy to new information which will challenge every truth you currently accept as fact, as well as your whole concept of what reality is.

If a group, species if you wish, were to be told the truth as it is known to a vastly more aware group of beings, not only would it literally blow your minds but it would also significantly disrupt the balance and energetic flow of everything in existence. So it is because of this you are drip fed in such a way that balance, harmony, and flow continues to, well, flow.

Think of it as the greatest science experiment imaginable. How exciting each breakthrough is, each new definable, provable, undeniable fact that leads to greater awareness and understanding.

The more tuned in a group's vibrational frequency is in relation to Source Energy the easier this becomes and more rapidly takes place.

The greater awareness becomes, the less resistance is offered, and therefore the group advances at an ever-increasing rate until it doesn't need to anymore.

The most advanced thinkers, philosophers, theologians and scientists that exist within your group all have, and ask, various questions on a vast array of subjects. One of which is seeking proof of the meaning and purpose of your existence.

We would say to them that applying various aspects of each discipline would lead you closer to your goals. Therefore work together without bias or resistance to each-others views, ideas, thoughts, and feelings but rather with an acceptance, an *open-mindedness that will lead you all to an immeasurable leap forward on your evolutionary journey.*

May peace, light, and love be with you all every step of the way.

Why do we act so separated from one another?

It is true that there is a large disconnection, more in some than others, from the light and truth of Spirit.

This has gradually been reducing over millennia within your realm and it is now at a crucial point where there will either be a large scale mass awakening, or you will destroy yourselves and start again, as has happened before.

There have been many cycles of this process which is known as cyclical evolution.

You have previously mastered peace and harmony then ascended into a more evolved realm. Now it is the turn of other souls to experience, learn and ascend to Source.

What you are currently experiencing is simply a phase of the cyclical evolution which will continue until it reaches its conclusion. Souls who have previously experienced this are standing by you, assisting and guiding you through your journey.

Some of these souls walk among you as they have chosen to return to the physical realm of Earth because of a great and pure love for you all. These beings are highly evolved and closer to Source so they may be of greater service to you. We exist in the main to love, to experience and to serve for no reward other than to do so for love's sake.

So in answer to your question, you have simply forgotten who you are and why you exist.

It is not to be successful in your career, or to gain control over others and your environment. It is not to cause harm, suffering or discontent. It is not to be rich or poor, gluttonous or hungry, right or wrong.

These are simply aspects of experience. You exist purely from love and for love, so that it may expand with the great cosmic breath.

If you tap into the deepest, most truthful part of yourself, you will know that your basic instinct is not of survival or competition, but of love.

To tip the balance of the great awakening, make every act, thought, feeling and word come from the place of pure love which exists within you. In each moment we urge you to be aware, to choose love and allow the light of Spirit to illuminate this world.

It is a simple choice which you have the free will to make.

Each soul may choose it for themselves but may not enforce it on others. Let your light shine brightly that others may see and know the way. And the way is love.

Do you see?

You look upon each other with the wrong eyes. The eyes of race, culture, and creed, the eyes of nationality, religious belief, gender and sexual preference.

As humans, you desire to label everyone and everything that you encounter, rather than just observing the beauty and wonder of creation which brought it to be. You have forgotten who you are and how to see, this is why you look with human eyes.

Let go of the need to label, to see differences for difference sake. Learn to see with the true eye which sees the truth, your inner eye.

Allow yourself to think, feel and comprehend, not with the physical brain, but rather with the heart-mind which connects you all. We have said this many times and we will say it again, you are spiritual beings having a human experience, not the other way round.

Think of each other in this way first and foremost, know that each spiritual being who walks with you in this physical experience comes from a place of pure love. You are all part of the eternal energy that exists eternally.

You are not your name, gender or belief system. You are not your nationality, your colour, your lifestyle or your sexuality.

Do not allow this to define you.

All of this is very human and you truly are not human.

All of these aspects of being exist to supply you with an experience so you may evolve and achieve a greater understanding of all that being entails, as well as allowing yourself to move through various vibrational frequencies.

We say to you now, observe all that is for what it seems to be, enjoy the magic of the experience and continue to evolve into the beautifully magnificent being that you are.

Know this;

All faces under the sun belong to the whole, the oneness that is. You are the sun and the moon, you are the galaxies and the stars within, you are everything that exists in every space that exists.

The sooner you understand you are not separate from anything, you are not different or alone, the sooner you will progress along your path of enlightenment.

We repeat this fact continuously, simply because there is a need to do so. Look around you and you will clearly see why. This truth must be repeated via countless sources, on innumerable occasions until it is accepted, remembered and known as the truth it is.

What's next for us as a people?

A storm is coming, there are turbulent times ahead. Many are raising awareness now, but it is not enough. A conscious choice needs to be made. You absolutely do have free will as do all beings in all the universes in existence.

What choice needs to be made?

Choose to move towards your own personal freedom.

The entrapment, suffering, and slavery you endure is com-
pletely self-imposed. You only need to choose to be free of these
bonds and you shall begin to enjoy a more harmonious, more
rewarding, fulfilling and peaceful existence.

Martin Luther King quoted to you, "Free at last, free at
last, thank God almighty we are free at last." There is great
truth in this but not in the way that would first come to mind.

As much as you can be free to express yourself in your exis-
tence, it is not God as a separate entity who will free you but
God who is you, who resides within, who will release you from
the bonds of restraint. For all the power of all that is, is you.

It is not an egocentric thought or belief that you are one and
the same as "the almighty" but a simple truth, that if known
beyond knowing would change your world forever.

What do you want to teach us?

Love.

Love, love and more love.

You have an abundance of everything on Earth, it is a spe-
cial place, yet you are lacking in love. It is the most powerful
energy in existence. Source is love in its purest, rawest form.

A love that is incomprehensible to you now but will not always be so. As you evolve through meditation, connection with spirit and reincarnation, you eventually attain a most peaceful, gentle, knowing of the ultimate truth of Sources love.

Are there any simple steps we can learn and teach?

Yes, slow down to speed up.

Take one single day to step back from your normal life or routine. For the entire day raise your awareness of everything around you, every aspect of every person, thing, sound, thought, feeling, smell, taste.

Observe every minute detail of everything and everyone you come in to contact with for that one day. Then before you go to sleep, sit quietly and observe yourself for a short time. How do you feel at that moment? Whatever the outcome, let yourself be grateful for the experience.

This is only a small selection of the questions I have had so far. If it has provided a different insight for you than what you previously held true, or given

you something positive to take from it, then I am truly grateful.

It is simply my interpretation based on my current
understanding of what is being relayed to me
through Spirit, which I am powerfully urged to share
for the evolution of our group.

CHAPTER THREE

Soul, Mind & Body

As a rule, we as humans really do love a label; be it a label for where you were born, which region you live in, what colour you are, which religion you follow, if any, what culture, which gender, the sexual preference you have, which diet you're on, which tax bracket you're in or which class within society and so on and so on. That's just in relation to us let alone everything that exists around us.

On the course of my journey, it has become my understanding that we are threefold beings, another label, at least while we exist in physical realms.

First and foremost we are spiritual beings, a tiny spark of the energy which is the Source of all things. Secondly, we have a mind, the one consciousness, where we process and record our experiences.

Finally, the body which we gain when we incarnate into the physical realm.

This chapter is about various aspects of all three, and these are some of my meditations relating to this threefold being experience.

Becoming a threefold being

You are your soul. You are a single entity, an eternal being of light who exists within the constructs of the 'ism'. Seemingly separated from Source, yet all the while deeply knowing the connection has never been broken but just extended out into the cosmos for you to experience all that is, until you come full circle and return to the oneness that you are.

When you incarnate into the physical realms, you suddenly become a threefold being.

This is where it gets complicated.

Coming from the simplicity of the spirit realm you now find yourself having to experience a human mind and body and all that entails.

The body is simply the vehicle which carries your soul on this physical journey, and the mind is the engine that drives it. They are necessary components to assist you in knowing many aspects of experience, which enable you to evolve along your path of enlightenment.

You have had many lifetimes and taken many forms so far, with many more to come. The journey is timeless, the experiences innumerable and the destination forever ready for your return.

While you exist in physical form you should nourish your body with food and drink and feed your mind with information that creates greater knowing. Yet as you do so, remember first and foremost that you are a spiritual being.

Give generously to your soul by living a full life so you may gain evolution through the lessons of experience. Each life you live, wherever it may be, is chosen by you so you may come to know all aspects of all that is.

This is why you reincarnate many times over.

Becoming a messenger

I am deep in meditation as I feel a male energy step forward and begin to speak with me telepathically.

Time and space can be bent to your will, within what is permitted. All actions must stem from love, higher vibrational thoughts and desires.

The path is long, unending.

All things are possible for you on this path of enlightenment. Choose to follow it and watch the magic unfold.

Do not focus on the content or subject matter too much. You will simply share what you are given as it is given. The more you do it, the more you trust and flow, the easier it will get.

His voice changes and suddenly becomes loud and stern.

Watch the magic unfold, appreciate how it takes place, observe and be aware, this will bring you (his tone softens) *great joy.*

Awakening is wonderful. Are you ready for your heart to expand? To feel the light and love of Spirit in all its glory? You are going to find yourself smiling a great deal!

What is, 'it'?

The messages, the information, the instructions, words, knowledge, wisdom and love.

Allow yourself to be your true self. The one you have always known yourself to be yet were too out of sync to allow before now. You have been through much learning and now you are ready to fulfill your purpose.

Dedicate yourself to this purpose, allow it to be your sole focus in this life. It will bring about great change, great love and the great light of Spirit will shine brightly amongst you all.

What is my path exactly?

Your path is to be a messenger, to share light, to illuminate the people of your world. You will do this by connecting with Spirit and allowing us to speak through you. You need not concern yourself with what will be said, as we will provide all that is needed for the highest good.

Continuing with this subject, I asked the following question in a different meditation. I don't remember the exact date but it was sometime between 1st May to 11th Jul 2018.

What's next for me?

Cast the stone into the water. Take the next step.

The next step is speaking publicly, sharing knowledge from Spirit, bringing light. Trust us to provide opportunities for you. Be aware and be ready to take them for they will come into your awareness soon.

It will not feel forced, but gentle and smooth. Slowly, slowly you will move forward and transition into more spiritual work.

Your focus will be on sharing the light of Spirit and empowering people to release themselves from self-imposed bonds. Strengthen your connection with us by meditating and having Spirit in your mind each day.

Be ready to work at any given moment. Fill yourself with the white light of Source Energy every day. Come to know us, know the truth and share it.

It is no good for one of you or even one million of you to be mediums, rather it is better that all of you have the ability and use it to free yourselves, so you may experience peace and harmony in the physical realm as well as the spiritual realms.

It is part of the common journey, you will have fun along the way, allow yourself to have fun and be playful.

I saw three symbols at this point, a heart, obviously symbolising love, a dollar sign which for me is a symbol for abundance and a large S surrounded by light which represented Source Energy. I believe the message they were giving me was this.

Share abundantly the love and light of Source which resides within, for there is an abundance available to be shared and received

Becoming more

Two major financial drains on society are war and healthcare. As you become more in tune with the oneness that is, you will no longer desire war, as the fears you hold will dramatically dissipate.

You will also become aware of a truth you are unable to describe, that you can heal yourself without the need for doctors or medicine.

All of this will obviously reduce the need for armies, weapons manufacturers, pharmaceutical companies, insurance companies and many other entities that profit from suffering.

Change is coming.

We are in the next phase of the great awakening, so what's next?

People around the world, as in the masses, will become more intuitive.

They will begin to realise there is more to them than meets the eye in the reflection of the mirror each morning. They will receive stronger, more definable feelings about what can happen in the future, as well as predictions about their own and other people's lives.

It will happen often enough for their minds to become more open to receiving the light and love of Spirit.

They will desire to know more.

It shall become the largest part of their focus, which will in turn remove, or at least reduce in some of you, the focus on selfishness, greed, lust, separation, loneliness, anger, hate, corruption, malice as well as many other low vibrational states of being.

Human beings will generally become kinder, gentler and more thoughtful, regarding themselves and all those they come into contact with. This is a major part of the worldwide shift in consciousness you will experience together.

As this occurs, you will observe a plainly noticeable difference in friends, family and society at large.

Although there will be those who offer resistance to this transition, they shall not be able to inhibit it. It is their role to simply provide contrast and balance for your awareness so you can more clearly define who you are becoming individually and as a whole.

In the darkest of darkness

In the darkest of darkness, in the most silent of silence, it is there you discover the very essence of life. Love! Love for your-

self, love for everything that you come into contact with, love which flows harmoniously, endlessly. A love which enables you to take each step on your path towards your goal of fulfilling your purpose and assisting with the evolution of the oneness that is. You and everything you can possibly comprehend is a vital part of this oneness.

Dreams

Dreams are the postmen of the spirit realm. They deliver important information and knowledge through symbols that have a definitive meaning. Love letters that reassure you in a supportive, caring way. Pay attention to your dreams. Aborigines didn't place significant importance on Dreamtime for nothing.

People

Humans want answers, facts, verifiable information that describes, in detail, all known things.

For example; Who is God? What is God? Prove God exists. Prove God does not exist. Who am I? Where did we come from? How did we evolve? And so many more questions.

Firstly, all information is available through ascension. The more you evolve, the more you know.

Secondly, there are no words to describe what you think of as "God" in any of your religions which adhere to a single, or multiple deity idea.

There are no words because there are no words there.

Words only exist in realms where the current state of group evolution is at a stage that requires them so the group can function at that particular stage.

There are realms where there is no time and space let alone words. The truth of this is not comprehensible to you at this stage. Try to understand that it is a state of simply knowing, a state of "ism."

For now, your focus should be on helping each other to evolve to the point where you exist in harmony with each other and with all that surrounds you. Nature, the universe, all that is.

Resolve your current state of being through connection with your true self, connecting with other beings of light and employing the knowledge, wisdom and love which is shared, to create a harmonious physical realm that can exist without the need to experience negative or low vibrational aspects of being.

There will truly come a stage where there is no longer any need to experience pain, suffering, hardship, greed, lust, anger, hate, revenge or separation of any kind, at least not within your group.

It will be enough to know that it exists elsewhere in the universe and you will go on to assist those groups in their evolution as you have been assisted in yours.

We would say to you, appreciate the process, the journey, as much as the destination. For without the former, the latter cannot be reached.

Ego

Unshackle the burdens which cause you to stumble and fall. You are the warden and the inmate in the prison of your mind. Yet you are able to release yourself at any moment by simply choosing to let go.

Let go of negative, low vibrational thoughts, feelings and emotions. Become the master of your ego, learn to control it and release it, release its' grip on you.

The ego has many faces, it is a wily creation that can easily mislead and confuse you; even the smartest among you.

For the ego knows it has no power over you other than that which you give. It knows this power can be removed in an instant should you so choose.

Recognise, acknowledge and observe all that the ego causes you to think, feel and emote.

Focus on each aspect, give it matter so that you may see it in the palm of your hand, then simply release it to the universe. Watch it dissipate before you.

Move through each low vibrational thought, feeling and emotion in this way.

This process will create a void which must be filled by law of the universe. Therefore we encourage you to seek out higher vibrational thoughts, feelings and emotions such as joy, happiness, laughter, wonderful health and wellness. Cleanse your physical self with appropriate foods and drinks but also remember to cleanse your soul with Spirit's light through meditation.

Ask yourself, 'what causes me to feel joy and happiness?' Think on these things, allow the answers to this question to flow to you, tune yourself to the vibrational frequency of these things. Seek out that which causes you to laugh until you cry.

Observe how these things make you feel in the moment you are feeling them. Once it is known, you may recreate joy and happiness whenever you desire.

Think about what makes you happy.

Add feelings and emotions to these thoughts and you shall observe an increase in your vibrational frequency. This will be as pleasing to us as it is to you, for you already know we are all connected, so what makes you happy, makes us happy.

Isn't it wonderful how pleasing it is?

Feel it, know it, become it. Think happy, feel happy, become happy.

Mental Illness

Mental illness and trauma, PTSD, depression and many other aspects of mental health, are all a disruption in the energy flow between the human mind and the soul. It is simply an out of tune vibration resonating on a lower frequency.

To correct it you must raise your vibration and re-tune the frequency to which you have become set. You can do this through meditation, visualisation and attuning yourself to things for which you can be grateful.

When you feel grateful, you feel happy, which is a higher vibrational state. So, as long as you exist in that moment of happiness, you cannot, in that very moment, simultaneously exist in a low vibrational state of misery, depression, self-loathing, trauma and ungratefulness.

It will take effort, self-discipline and focus in the beginning but in time you will realign yourself with your true vibrational frequency.

The wide range of mental illnesses truly is caused by a disruption in vibrational frequency. Either by choice of experience or external trauma. Find your way to re-tune yourself.

There are those who can help you heal and realign. You may seek them out but only you can choose to heal yourself.

It will be your conscious choice to do so.

Yes, you can be guided, but in the end, it is up to you to choose the path, the journey, the experience that you wish to have.

Balance your chakras, cleanse your energy fields, cleanse your soul with Spirit's light.

Seek out your guides, feel yourself becoming realigned with your true higher self. Cleanse your pineal gland with white light and allow yourself to expand.

Look not with your human eyes but with your inner eye. What do you see? What do you feel about what you see? What do your instincts tell you? Expand into the knowledge that you will come to see, feel and know.

Focus your energies on this, on healing yourself and others. For you know their pain, their quiet suffering, often hidden from view but always present.

Help them to release themselves from the slavery of their mind, so they may exist in the freedom of their soul.

The way is blessed, the way is truth, light and love.

Healing

Healing is done by the self. I am not here to heal you but to share the message, the knowledge that you are, and always have been, able to heal yourself.

If you get a small cut on your arm, do I come to you and heal it? Does a doctor come to your home? No, your body heals itself. As is the case with all things.

This is a controversial thought to your group but one that is true and becomes a reality once you evolve to the point that you remember and comprehend who you are.

In the meantime, medical care, traditional and holistic, provides a process which is required by you for the purpose of experiential learning. Remember it is only your body and organs that require healing, not your soul.

Your soul is perfect, it is free of all illness, all disease and imperfections. The saying you have "nobody is perfect" is so very true. For it is not your body that defines you, but your soul and your souls' experiences. It is the pureness and truth which is the absolute essence of who you are.

Whilst existing in the physical realm you must follow, work with, the physical laws as you understand them to be in this moment.

That's not to say those laws or the understanding of them won't change in future but in each moment you must exist within your current comprehension.

These laws can be played with, bent to your will, as others who have come before you have shown and as other beings who co-exist in the present moment with you have come to know.

However, this can only be achieved if the desire to do so comes from a place of love, pure love, Spirit's Love.

What is the pineal gland and how do we access it?

The next meditation I will share with you was going to be in Chapter Two. It relates to one of the questions that I mentioned receiving before, but because it relates to a gland that is located in our physical brains, I thought it would be appropriate here as it links the body beautifully with the soul and all that is.

The pineal gland or what you commonly refer to as your third eye, is how the physical being gains access to the spiritual realm whilst remaining in a physical state of being. It is an important aspect of the journey.

You must move to the beat of a different drum. Retune yourself, alter your vibration.

Everything has a vibrational frequency, every thing. All that is tuned to the common frequency flows harmoniously with all that is.

You achieve this through meditation and gradually altering your perception of reality. You will become aware of symbols, you will hear thoughts, you will feel Spirit and know the truth.

This process alters your perspective, your understanding of the reality of what is, through increased awareness of the knowledge that is shared with you.

Imagine a pure white light filling up the pineal gland, gradually growing or expanding.

The intensity of this light increases until it is as bright as your sun, to the point that you would logically think it should burn your brain from the inside out, yet there is no heat.

You feel and internally see the light expanding throughout your physical brain; each synapse, each avenue, every neuron is filled, encompassed by this light and at once you feel truly connected with the whole.

Constantly maintaining this activation is a learned process. You learn by intuitively sensing what the pineal gland allows you to see. You enhance the ability and strength of this gland by choosing regular meditation and by reducing or removing fluoride from your life to decalcify the pineal gland.

Although we would say to you that removing fluoride and or following a plant-based diet is good for you in the physical sense, it is only a short-term solution; for when you come to know beyond knowing, to be truly connected to your higher self, you will realise that you create your experience and you truly create every aspect of that experience

Be it purifying your toothpaste, cleansing the food and water you consume or activating the pineal gland, keeping it activated and using it for the betterment of all.

So, why do it? Why use this gland?

First of all, it helps you to see the truth of creation. It will help you to expand your knowledge and understanding of all that is. How quickly this takes place depends on how far you have come along the path of your journey of evolution.

You will then desire to share what you have seen and learned. You are welcome to do this but the greatest under-

standing can only come from the self experiencing the self as it truly is.

Your aim should be to attain consistent activation and connection with Spirit via the pineal gland, third eye. All the Ascended Masters have done this before you.

Then not only share what you see, learn and know but also teach others how to do the same and be accepting of what comes next; revelation.

This can be hard on the less evolved among you, so they will need greater care, guidance, and healing. Share this ability, share this light, love and healing with all you come into contact and observe the beauty and magic of Spirit being unveiled before your eyes, causing greater evolution of souls in all realms. What a joy to behold this is.

Key point: Link pineal gland, third eye, to the physical self via the central nervous system, then every instinctive thought, feeling, and action will be led by Spirit. Visualise the connection, allow yourself to feel it happening and accept it as simply as you accept breathing.

The nature of being

The nature of a thing is to evolve, to blossom and grow. To become more than it once was, so it may know more, be more and enhance the whole that is connected to it.

Life exists to become self-aware; to experience itself as itself in a particular experience. Knowing and experiencing are two different things.

You cannot only know Spirit exists. You must also experience Spirit. You do this by becoming connected through meditation, waking up to your true consciousness, engaging with your higher self, remembering who you are and how you exist in true reality.

Awareness is the lock of experience in the door of understanding.

Remember this as it is a big step on the path of enlightenment for each and every soul. Once you bring the two together you will remember all that you are.

Every aspect of every experience is available to you, nothing is held back or hidden.

All is a choice; your choice.

For you are the true creator of your reality, your experience in existence. The purpose of all of this is the unending evolution and devolution of all things. This is cosmic breathing.

(Key point, evolution = expansion. You exist to devolve, experience, evolve, remember, devolve, experience, evolve remember and devolve for as long as is desired.)

Karma

(Sometimes when I meditate or work with Spirit, they will give me a word. For each letter of that word I will either get another word or a sentence which will lead to a message for myself or another person at the time. This is what happened during a meditation one Sunday afternoon when I asked Spirit about Karma.)

Know the truth
Align with the truth
Receive the true gifts
Messages of light
Allow healing, understanding and evolution of the soul

Know the truth of all that is spoken, of all which is seen and that you have felt. Instinctively align yourself with the truth of this to receive the true gifts of Spirit. The messages of light which allow hope, peace and understanding to flourish in the microcosm of your soul as well as the macrocosm of the whole. This, in turn, will bring healing which leads to acceptance of the truth that is so all who know may evolve and continue to do so.

Karma is the spiritual belief of cause and effect. There are four religions of which I am aware which speak about Karma: Buddhism, Hinduism, Jainism and Sikhism.

My current knowledge of these religions is limited at best but suffice to say they have deep thoughts and teachings about this subject in relation your actions and those of others, as well as reincarnation.

In many cultures and throughout popular belief, when you perceive someone has wronged you and you either choose not to act or feel powerless to do so, Karma will be your go-to instrument of revenge, payback or poetic justice.

"Karma will get them, what goes around comes around, they'll get what's coming to them, if not in this life then the next" and so on. During the nature of being meditation I received a message about Karma and this is my interpretation of that message.

Karma is a being choosing to experience a particular event in a future incarnation for their own, and our, evolution. It is not a weapon of vengeance to be used by anyone or anything.

There is no reward or punishment in life or the afterlife.

All beings exist to provide and receive experience to facilitate evolution. That is why so-called good things, bad things and everything in between happens.

When you incarnate as a physical being, your vibration naturally lowers compared to when you are in your true spiritual state, to enable this process to occur. For this reason, when you have your experiences as a physical being, particularly the "bad" ones, they can be harder to comprehend.

No matter the event or the part you play, you will at some point be every aspect of every experience. When you remember who you are and begin to connect with your higher self as well as Source Energy you will have a greater understanding and a broader perspective that puts all things, good and bad, into perspective.

This, in turn, brings peace to your soul.

The stronger the connection you have with your spiritual self whilst in the physical realm, the more you will be able to feel and know this peace in your current life.

Make time to breathe, to meditate, to be consciously aware of the moment you are in. We all start somewhere, so do not be afraid to move beyond each experience; to learn the lessons, to evolve to a new state of being.

You are who you are in each moment. This is your truth in that exact moment. Yet in the very next moment, there is the possibility of a new truth.

The truth is only true as you accept it to be within your current comprehension, so know it is you who chooses each and every truth of each and every experience you have along your evolutionary journey.

In that, there is ultimate truth.

CHAPTER FOUR

Many lives lived

So much has been written, spoken about, taught and handed down anecdotally about reincarnation. There is lots of evidence, easily found online, that suggests we all have many lives.

I've read books, articles, watched videos, podcasts and had conversations where the most unlikely of people have told me about their own past life experiences, or at least the suspicion that they have lived on earth before.

I have also been fortunate enough to take part in guided past life regression sessions at the psychic circle I attended and discovered a few of my own past lives.

When doing the past life regression I was told to try and be aware of as much detail as possible;

where I was; the year; what I was wearing; how I looked; how I felt; what could I see around me and what I was doing at the time.

Not long into the recollection of each life, I'd be asked to jump forward 20 years and describe everything again, then finally move on to my death and describe all that I could about it. Here is a selection of lives that I have been able to recall.

Past life regression; session one:

First life;

I see an ink pot on a gently lit table and I am sat there writing by candlelight. It is a letter or message for someone, it is a warning of betrayal. I am wearing a helmet, a Roman centurion's helmet.

The year is 22AD. I am alone in a tent. I don't know what country I'm in but it feels like a foreign country to me. It is not my homeland.

Skip forward twenty years.

Everything is blank. I am dead.

I feel as though I was murdered after writing the letter. I had a strong sense of betrayal in this life, so the lesson is to let go of the betrayal I feel in my present life. I find myself moving into a tunnel and on to the next life in the session.

Second life;

I am a General in China. I am in my late thirties and the year is around 103-105AD. It is a time of war and hardship.

There is a woman in the distance. She's holding a parasol of some sort. She is my lover and was an influence on my conscience. Her energy feels familiar. The realisation comes to me that it's Julia and we are sharing another incarnation together.

I am in a temple. It is an open space and I am in a meeting with several people of significant importance; a kind of council meeting where big and difficult decisions are being made.

I am visibly stressed by the enormity of the responsibility of my position. These decisions will affect many people greatly and it is weighing heavily on me.

Skip forward twenty years.

I'm in my late fifties and living on a farm; working, harvesting crops. I don't see anyone else with me. I am now living a much simpler and more peaceful life but my mind is a different story.

It is full of difficult memories which cause me unrest. The actions and consequences of my youth still haunt me and are etched on my face.

I don't see or feel anything about my death here so I gently come out of the meditation.

Past life regression; session two
First life;

I am a woman and my name is Katherine. I am quite young; early to mid-twenties and pretty with blonde hair but my features are hardened by life.

I'm wearing a blue dress with a white apron and a white bonnet. My face is dirty and there is blood splattered over my apron. I am a nurse in Britain in the Middle Ages.

There is a man with me. His name is Arthur. He is handsome with brown hair, a full beard and a strong brow. I look around and notice I am on a battlefield. As I take in my surroundings, the man, Arthur, gently leaves me.

I feel as though Arthur was a spirit guide who was there to help me through quite a traumatic lifetime.

Skip forward twenty years.

I don't see or feel anything so assume that I have already died but I have no recollection of how.

I believe I incarnated as her to understand the brutal effects of war and to help the victims of it so I could gain a different perspective of acts carried out in other lives.

For example, decisions I made causing war to occur or actions carried out which brought about great suffering of numerous people.

Second life;

I am a man of about thirty years old. I'm wearing a tunic and sandals. I am ex-military and currently a politician. The year is 892AD, I'm standing on a hill looking out across the countryside. I am not sure of the country but it feels like ancient Greece or Rome.

My wife is in the background (it's Julia again - she's been with me in several lifetimes) her role was to guide me in having more compassion for people; even those who mean you harm, such as enemies and political opponents.

Skip forward twenty years.

I am a political leader of my country surrounded by enemies who feel like snakes, vipers. I had to be strong and stick to my beliefs.

Spirit was encouraging me to let go of my human thoughts, feelings, emotions and remember my true self so that I may bring about the highest good for all. During the regression I feel Spirit speak to me;

To disconnect from that which makes you human is to reconnect with your soul. It is then that you shall evolve to a higher vibration and be closer to the reality of truth.

Past life regression; session three

First life;

I am a fifty-year-old male sitting in a tea house in China. I am wearing black boots and a cloak. The year is 327BC.

My son from my current life is with me in this life. He is my brother and a Lieutenant in my army. I am his General. I tried to protect him from battle but he died anyway. I am devastated by his loss.

Skip forward twenty years.

I am at my home walking with my sheep, solitary again.

I feel Spirit say to me; *the controller can't be controlled.*

I could not control the outcome of my brothers' destiny, as he chose his experience. I need to let go of control and allow people to have the experience they came to have.

Second life;

Again I am male. I am thirty-eight years old and it is 1841AD. I have brown hair and a thick moustache. I am wearing black leather shoes, a top hat and tails and am sitting in a horse-drawn carriage.

I am deep in thought about the loss of my wife and child during the birth. I am a top surgeon yet I am filled with regret that I could not save my own family.

Skip forward twenty years.

I see and feel nothing more about this life. I am dead again.

Clarity

When I meditate there are times when what I receive from Spirit is not always clear to me, or I may misinterpret it somewhat. However, at some point in the future, it is made clearer to me with gentle love and patience.

An example of this was a past life regression back in March 2016 along with a meditation I did over two years later in August 2018. These meditations were cleared up for me only today, 15th Feb 2019, as I sit here writing this chapter on a cold, wet, wintery day in North Cyprus.

Let me start with the past life regression session; I am male; 18 years old. I have a light olive skin tone. I am wearing sandals and a tunic with a brown belt around my waist.

I am not sure of the exact year but it's very far back in time; more than 3000 years ago.

I am in a temple and there is a sea God idol in front of me. I stand and gaze at it for a moment as priests and priestesses pass me by, going about their business.

It is day time. I can see through an entrance to the temple that the sun is shining brightly outside. It is a warm day. I feel as though I am possibly in Atlantis.

Skip forward twenty years.

I am a solitary person. I have become a scholar of ancient knowledge and wisdom.

I am outside the temple. There is an enormous volcanic eruption which causes mass destruction and many people are dying all around me.

I begin to run but suddenly I feel an almighty force lift me off my feet and throw me through the air. I know I am about to die and I am filled with regret.

I regret that I did not fulfill my purpose and share the knowledge that was so generously shared with me.

The lesson from this life is to have the confidence to share the knowledge that has been handed down to me. I leave now and enter a tunnel of light.

As you have just read, I thought I was a student in a temple in Atlantis more than 3000 years ago. I really wasn't sure of the location although I was sure it was a warm, sunny day by the sea. The volcanic eruption was also very clear, as was my subsequent death.

So, skipping forward to August 2018, I am on holiday in Greece with my wife and son.

It is a warm summer's afternoon and we are currently on a ferry in Crete sailing through the beautiful blue waters of the Aegean. Sat here surrounded by fellow tourists, who are overtired from a long day's hike through the awe-inspiring Samaria Gorge,

I decided to meditate while everyone around me slept peacefully.

Why am I in Crete?

To see. See the old ways. Sometimes you have to go back to the beginning to know where you are going. This is where it all started for you (ancient Greece). Your first incarnation in Greece over 3,000 years ago in your time. You have come full circle by coming back to the first life on your journey. You have incarnated many times. Now you have come back to remember, to reconnect with yourself and your true purpose. To share.

I ask why I was shown Aristotle in a previous meditation, in which he said; *seek me out in mainland Greece and Crete.* It was because of this meditation that we felt compelled to visit Greece on this holiday. I felt him draw close to me. He stepped forward and gently answered;

We were friends once, teacher and student, yet we taught each other in many ways.

I drew you back to Greece, as I promised I would, in case you had forgotten who you are and why you are here.

Remember now, my friend. Remember who you are and help them to do the same. Have the courage to step forward and do your duty. You are on the path already, just remember the way.

Awaken brother! Wake up and know yourself.

On my first visit to Athens during this holiday we visited the Lyceum. An ancient meeting place for philosophical debate which later became a school where Aristotle would teach.

Whilst walking around trying to connect with the energy there, I stopped at a far corner of the site, reached out and lay my hand on one of the uncovered original walls.

I closed my eyes and was shown that in this place Angels had walked closely amongst men in those times; whispering words of wisdom and inspiration to the teachers and students that they would later share as philosophical teachings.

I started to get the impression I had actually been a young athlete in this life and had grown an interest in philosophy, mainly thanks to Aristotle of course.

Whilst standing there, with my physical eyes firmly closed, I looked down with my third eye and saw that my hand, wrist and part of my forearm no longer had its physical appearance but was now an intensely bright golden/white light of pure energy.

I had for the first time been shown my higher self in my true form.

It was an incredible moment which left me awestruck and grateful. What an amazing privilege to be connected in such a way.

I decided to look up the volcanic eruption which had been such a clear aspect of the past life regression and it turns out there was one of the largest volcanic eruptions in history over 3000 years ago. It was known as "The Minoan eruption in Thera" (now called Santorini).

The exact date is disputed somewhat, by around a hundred years, but it still gave me enough validation to realise that I was actually in Greece and that it was likely I was studying Atlantis, rather than being in Atlantis itself.

I don't know why but I had never thought to look it up before today but as I go through this journey I begin to see more and more that everything happens at the right time for the highest and best good, or at least the greatest effect.

The information in front of me, the intuitive feeling inside me, along with the gentle way in which the realisation flowed to me all combined to give me clarity.

Under the tree at the Acropolis

Another meditation relating to past lives I would like to share with you was a brief one I did whilst visiting the Acropolis in Athens.

If you haven't been I suggest you go as pictures and videos don't really do it justice.

It was a hot summer's day so once we reached the top and had explored a little I decided to seek some shade and see if I could tune in to the energy of the place.

With so many tourists around the general noise was quite a distraction for someone who is still relatively new to meditation so I was happy to find that I could not only tune in, but also have an interaction with my former self who had sat here thousands of years ago.

I see people in robes, mainly men. They're coming to worship the Gods. I become aware of myself sitting under the shade of a tree, resting my head against it and contemplating, exactly as I am doing right now in my current physical life.

I've been here before. I was a philosopher. At this point, the being that I was in this previous life spoke quietly to me;

I have seen so many people pass by, lost in their own worlds, not understanding the power, beauty and magic of who they really are, or the power, beauty and magic of all that surrounds them.

They have no understanding of the intricacies of the universe; of how it all works and comes together to create the wonder and magic of life. I most desired to see people realise the truth of this; to become aware, to free themselves from the prison of their own minds.

Happiness to me is simply being. That is to say being in the moment, appreciating the beauty and magnificence of life, of people and of our connection with each other and the universe. I, we, had once known, forgotten and been taught again how to love each other in the proper way.

Now it seems we have forgotten once more and in turn, caused separation within the self and from each other. We must remember how to love, to reconnect with our true self, with each other and remember our true purpose which is twofold.

Firstly, to remember who we truly are and observe our experience to assist in our own evolution.

Secondly, to discover and carry out assistance to those
around us for the evolution of all creation.
Find a way to appreciate and be grateful for the journey.
Now discover once more the magic, beauty and truth of exis-
tence.

Why bother?

I've often heard people say, "If it's so wonderful in
the afterlife, why bother coming to earth and being
human at all? Why let yourself suffer?"

Well, for a start, it's not all about suffering; at least
not in every lifetime. There are plenty of good experiences to be had along the way. What I present in
this book is simply my interpretation and comprehension of the experiences I have had so far which I
know can deepen, change and evolve over time.
What I will say is this, as was mentioned in the nature of being at the end of the last chapter, "You

cannot only know Spirit exists, you must experience Spirit".

In order to know all physical things, we incarnate so that we can experience all aspects of creation in the physical realms. We experience every aspect from every point of view, so that we may evolve to a greater point of knowing which can only come through experience.

How can you truly know physical pain unless you are physically hurt? How can you truly know emotional pain unless your heart is broken through loss?

How can you know love unless you feel love, for a lover or as a parent to a child or simply for your fellow beings?

How can you possibly know the difference between these unless you experience both?

For without darkness you cannot know light. Without pain you will never know the power of healing. Without sadness you will not truly appreciate joy and this in part is why "good" and "bad" things happen.

So this is why we bother and why there is a purpose to everything in life, death, reincarnation and everything in between.

CHAPTER FIVE

Guides, Angels & Masters

This is a particularly special subject for me. I think many of us can relate to an experience regarding interactions with these beautiful beings of divine light and love.

Even people who haven't knowingly had an experience with them seem to have a desire to connect, to know who your guide is or Guardian Angel is.

Then there are the Ascended Masters who are able to enlighten us in many beautifully wise and loving ways, either from the spirit realm or sometimes over here in the physical plain.

We all have a collective of beings who work closely with us throughout each life we live, they are known as our "Spirit group".

To begin this chapter I'd like to share my current group with you. I say current as these beings come and go at various stages of each individual's journey to assist their evolution. My desire is that this will create an urge within you to connect to or deepen your relationship with your own group.

My Spirit Group

Spirit Guides
Names:

- Hunter
- Chief
- Bobby

Guardian Angels:

- Archangel Gabriel
- Archangel Raphael

Ascended Masters:

- Jesus
- Simon

I believe there have been other Masters who have worked with me but I do not know what to call them. They haven't given me a name of any sort as names aren't as relevant or important to them as they seem to be to us.

When I connect with my guides they give me impressions, symbols, feelings and a quiet sense of knowing that they are with me.

With Hunter, I will generally see a large eagle and know he is close. He has a fairly young appearance. I would place him at mid-twenties. He is slightly taller than me (which isn't hard) and he has strong features, a plaited ponytail at the upper rear part of his shaved head, an athletic slightly muscular frame and his energy usually feels quite strong and stern.

Yet at times there is a softness to him that I feel when we blend our energies in my meeting place. He is the guide that has been with me the most over the last few years and I have relied on his strength and support on more than one occasion during that time.

When I see a big native American head-dress I know that Chief is with me.

My guides aren't into names so I assign my own to them, with their permission, as it helps me when communicating with them, as well as speaking or writing about them.

He is older than Hunter and has a fuller frame. I don't know how tall he is as he's usually sitting down when I see him. He has a jovial way about him. He reminds me of the laughing Buddha. I also sense he is an incredibly wise and philosophical being.

I don't see or feel him with me as often as Hunter but I know that he is available to me whenever I need him and invite him to draw close.

Bobby is an Australian Aboriginal guide who I've only seen twice. He is tall with a solid frame and has dark brown skin, black curly hair and soft features. He's very relaxed and has a warm smile.

I know that we will connect more in the future but it isn't the right time. It was more of a brief introduction so that I'm aware of his presence for when the moment comes.

Archangel Gabriel is harder for me to describe. I have never seen a physical manifestation of him. I get more of a feeling of love when he's with me.

I have the stereotypical image of Angels that I've learned to have over the years: large beings with wings and bright auras around them.

I often feel him wrapping his wings around me and when he does so I get a wonderful sense of profound love and protection. I simply know that when he is with me I will be safe. I will never be alone and I am loved beyond comprehension.

My other Guardian Angel is Archangel Raphael, the healer.

When he draws close I sense the colour jade around me. Again, I have never seen a physical manifestation of him, I only feel his presence, his energy, with me. It is a beautifully powerful yet gentle energy that not only physically heals but comforts you in a way that only an Angel could.

What an absolute blessing it is to know and to feel this energy flow through you.

I have worked with various Ascended Masters in the last few years, most of whom haven't given me a name to call them by. They seem to step forward, share a message or teaching and then leave again. However, one who I feel connects with me more regularly is Jesus.

I feel as though I have a strong bond with him. I still haven't remembered why as yet but I know that it will become clear at the perfect moment.

There are, of course, many images of him throughout various cultures in our societies but I have not yet seen him with either my physical eyes or my inner eye. What I do see is a beautifully power-ful-looking Stag in a forest. This is the symbol that represents him for me. Other times I will simply feel him, as though his energy has a distinct signature which lets me know beyond doubt who is with me.

The first time he drew close to me I remember thinking I was half crazy; half like a star-struck fan meeting his favourite celebrity.

I was nervous, overawed and full of disbelief, telling myself, 'this isn't happening, that can't be Jesus'. Asking myself and Spirit, why would Jesus want to talk to me? Have I finally lost the plot?

I thought meditation was supposed to be relaxing! I am *not* feeling relaxed right now.

I was a mess, until the moment he drew close, laid his hand on my chest and said lovingly;

Know that it is me.

In that instant I felt my heart expand and fill with pure love. My mind simultaneously became quiet, calm and at peace with the interaction between us.

I have reached the point now where I can accept gratefully the guidance, wisdom and love he generously shares with me.

Another Ascended Master with whom I have interacted is Simon.

It is hard to put into words who and what Simon truly is. He told me in meditation that regardless of the form he takes or the name he uses, he has an energetic signature that remains the same.

Most true to say is that he is a wonderfully wise, highly evolved, limitless being who is as gentle as he is powerful.

When he is near I get a feeling of depth, reverence and magic in the true sense of the word. Then there is the cold rush, the goosebumps and the expansion of my soul's energy brought just by being close to him.

I hope that you will all have and continue to know the privilege of connecting with this truly magnificent being of light and love.

About Angels

I have often wondered about Angels. In my childhood I asked for their help many times but I never received it, or so my out of tune mind thought, so I gave up and to some degree lost hope.

In my early twenties, without having the first clue what I was doing, I attempted to communicate with them after following some guidelines which I thought I'd randomly come across in a magazine. I did not realise back then that there are no random occurrences or coincidences.

I was unsuccessful at the time; partly due to not knowing what I was doing and partly because I was trying too hard to force something to happen. I have since learned it's not the most conducive route to communicating with Angels.

I guess I've always been curious and since realising that I actually did have the ability to communicate with them, doing my best to get my ego out of the way, I've had many experiences with these beautiful, powerful, loving beings of light.

There have also been other Angels who have communicated with me and through me. Archangels Michael and Zadkiel, as well as many more Angels for whom I don't have names, have come through to give messages and healing to me and others.

My experience so far is very limited and I know I have a lot more to learn about them.

With so many preconceived ideas existing about these beings, I thought I'd ask them to explain in their own way about Angels.

Much has been said, written, painted and expressed about us, not just in your world. We would simply want you to know that we exist through love and with love for the ever-expanding light of Source.

We are yet another aspect of light; another part of Source Energy who created all things. There are seven main aspects to Angels:

1. Guide

2. Guardian

3. Warrior

4. Teacher/Prophet

5. Protector

6. Master

7. Healer

We are any one of these as and when it is required. At times we will be multiple aspects simultaneously.

Our purpose is to act as a bridge between the degrees or levels of evolution of all souls that exist; to enable remembrance so that we may eventually return to Source. We use means that are appropriate for each aspect in existence and our form depends on who or what we are assisting.

For humans, we have taken the form of winged human-like beings, as this is considered pleasing and comforting to you. At other times we have appeared in our truer form which is of light and pure energy.

There have been lights in the sky which you have assumed to be various celestial objects, even UFO's have actually been us in transition.

We are benevolent beings that draw close to you in times of need. We also observe dispassionately other aspects of your life and of all who exist on earth, such as those matters of greater significance to large groups of you. Natural disasters, war, famine, pollution and so on which can also affect you on your path.

We will communicate with you through thoughts, feelings, dreams, symbols and of course in mediation. When you see sparks of light from the corner of your eye, rest assured that you may know with all certainty it is us in your presence.

In your solar system, or more accurately, realm, we have our focus on you and on earth. However, there are other beings who have the ability to visit you quite frequently from other systems or realms. We also observe, assist and communicate with them .

They are generally curious travellers. They are observers who are more evolved and have no desire or need to cause harm to any beings in existence, especially you who are relatively primitive.

This primitive aspect of your group is changing more rapidly now than previously so we have drawn closer to you as the veil grows ever thinner between what you know and the true reality of all that exists.

The single most important thing for you to know about us right now is that we are beings of light and love who will never leave you, that we are always with you and will forever assist you on your chosen path until you no longer need us.

A bit about Masters

Ascended Masters are beings of light who move freely through time and space. There are no boundaries or limitations on them for they have evolved beyond any concept of boundaries that you may have.

They assist in large scale group evolution through various means. Etheric contact is made via dreams and meditation; physical contact through choosing to incarnate into human beings and other life forms on occasion.

They are able to coordinate planetary matters and have an influence on the outcomes of planet-wide concerns. Apart from simply being, their main focus is on teaching; on bringing messages through mediums or showing themselves to us whilst being incarnated amongst us in the physical realms.

They will speak of and demonstrate to us our true nature. Whether we listen and learn is another matter but they teach regardless.

Masters come in many forms.

I ask what message or teaching the Masters would have for all of us existing on earth right now.

Love.

You have forgotten that you are the energetic embodiment of love itself. You came from love and will return to it. Love is free and should be shared freely, generously and with a selflessness that reflects your true self.

You have all forgotten much about who and what you are but, above all, you have forgotten how to love each other.

You have been shown many, many times throughout the history of your planet and you have always forgotten. There is no judgement in this statement for it is the way of things. It has been the path of your group's spiritual evolution to do so.

However, the moment is upon you that brings the dawn of a new path. It is a step forward in the evolution of the entire group.

Jesus

I am sat with my wife in the snug, a spare room in our home that we use in the winter as a living room. The sound of our son watching cartoons in his room filters faintly through the wall as we prepare to meditate.

We close our eyes and breathe deeply. We pray and gently drift into a peaceful state of being. I invited my Guides, Guardian Angel and Ascended Masters to draw close to me.

Once more I head to my meeting place, take a seat and wait there for whoever should choose to come. I am there for quite some time and begin to feel as though there will be no message or interaction this time, which has happened before.

It doesn't bother me if that's the case as I use it as a time to relax and I'm grateful for the peace it brings me.

However, just as I am about to return, I feel an energy step forward. I see a beautiful large Stag in the distance. Instantly I know Jesus is here.

As previously mentioned, when we first interacted I felt overawed. I have also felt humbled and inspired in a very powerful way but this time was different.

Julia noticed it and asked me afterwards if this time felt more normal than usual, like two people just having a conversation. It had and it felt a little strange at first. There was just a very normal feeling about it, although I did still get goosebumps at various moments of the conversation.

I felt a question come to mind so I asked, 'why did you come to Earth and suffer the way you did?'

I have walked the Earth many times before my incarnation as Jesus. I have experienced many levels of joy and happiness as well as many levels of pain and suffering.

The pain and suffering during my torture and death as Jesus was a very advanced level of experience, only possible after a great journey of evolution.

I lived this life to help heal you, to help you to remember who you are and, in turn, live in peace and harmony with yourself and others. I came to help you remember how to love, both yourself and each other.

I did not come to teach you right from wrong or teach you about sin or piety. I wanted only for you to understand, to remember that everything I spoke about, every so-called miracle I showed you, every act of love I offered, that you could do all this and more.

I died for you, not to cleanse you of sin as there is no sin, only experience, but to assist in the evolution of us all.

I will come again, this time to live purely in joy, happiness and love.

There are many dark experiences occurring throughout your group which will be cleansed with a light so bright and a love so powerful that it cannot be resisted or denied.

You will all come to see the truth of what is; you will remember and you will know.

Do not despair, for suffering and hardship are but temporary aspects of the experience. Your love, light and soul energy are eternal. This is your truth.

Darkness simply provides contrast to the light. Have faith and trust that you will exist in this light once more. You will return home.

Guidance is being offered to those of you who are able to know it. I say to you now, share it for the betterment of all.

There are many within your group who are listening yet do not use this ability in the correct way. They share what is given but do so for the wrong reasons.

Share as I have shared with you. Help them to remember and offer guidance with this purpose in mind.

Teach them how so that they too may see, feel, hear and know the truth of who they are and all that is available to them. Let your light guide them to the path and give them the courage to travel upon it for at the end of this journey is truth and the truth shall set them free.

No more a slave of the mind, rather you re-emerge as the spark of life who moves freely throughout existence.

Regarding the many who are listening but do not share or use their ability in the correct way: I believe this is referring to those who give readings that focus on fortune telling.

They deal with questions about meeting someone new and possibly finding love, success, wealth, good health and happiness, in whichever order people prioritise them. It may also refer to connecting people with loved ones who have crossed over into the spirit realm.

They do this in person, online or over the phone using tarot cards, Angel cards, coffee or teacup readings, psychometry and many other tools that have a common thread; to connect with Spirit.

I am sure the intentions of almost all of the people giving the readings, working with the energies and so on are good as they want to help people and this desire comes from a place of love. I say almost all as I know there is a small minority of people in every walk of life who may possibly have less ethical motivations.

Giving readings in this way deserves respect because it is a beautiful blessing to be able to bring much needed light into our world. Whatever brings you to the point of awakening, whatever form it takes, whatever lights the spark of curiosity within you so that you seek to know more, can only be a good thing.

Once you start down that path, there really is no turning back. We all reach our destination via different routes but we do reach it all the same.

The point is that we should be teaching people how to connect with Spirit themselves. We all have this ability and should be using it to fulfill our own individual purpose, to evolve on our own journeys and then assist as many souls as we can to do the same.

I believe what is meant here is that we should be teaching each other how to remember the truth of who we are.

We do not need to leave physical aspects of being to chance, but we should remember that we are masters of all that is. So much so, in fact, that we are the ones who create our experience in such a powerful way that it can manifest before our very eyes to play out as we desire.

We should step into our magnificence safe in the knowledge that we are eternal beings of light who are not governed by physical laws but rather we are free beings that move throughout existence with one common purpose; to evolve until we return to that from which we came.

Simon

My first interaction with Simon in this form began with a question. I asked without knowing who would answer, 'how do I bring Source's light into this world?'

As I sat in meditation awaiting the answer I started to become aware of an image of a large erupting volcano. Extremely hot smoke, rock and lava are shooting up into the sky above and simultaneously oozing down the sides. I get the feeling that it signifies change, a new beginning.

At this point, I feel a powerfully wise being draw close. I get a shiver run down my spine and become covered in goosebumps. I am completely in awe of their presence as they begin to communicate with me.

Just speak and let the words flow for it is not you. The answers to the questions come from beyond you and your world.

For some reason, I want to ask him about aliens and before I can figure out why, he gently answers with a smile.

Yes, there are aliens; other beings; other worlds; other universes. All that you can think of and more is real.

They exist in their reality; in their time and space. Some exist without time as it does not exist with them. It is a lower vibrational concept, one that is no longer needed once you have evolved beyond it.

The words will flow like a runaway train, speeding through you, faster than you can fathom right now. You should know that you are always in control. It is simply that you do not as yet accept your potential or your truth.

Give in to the truth of yourself, of who and what you are. Let truth flow freely. Be the bridge between worlds, between peoples and dimensions. You are a link, one who brings us together and brings worlds together to facilitate the evolution of beings.

What do I tell them?

<u>You</u> tell them nothing. We will speak. We will explain. We will provide the words which you will simply translate into a

language they can grasp so there can be no doubt about what is being shared with them. We will speak a truth undeniable by all.

Who are you? The one who is communicating with me right now?

I am an evolved being. You would think of me as an ascended master. I walked your Earth millennia ago. You may refer to me as Simon.

He feels my confusion at such a 'normal' name and gently smiles as he continues:

Yes, Simon. I chose it as it was plain, simple, nothing out of the ordinary. What did you expect? Optimus Prime? Hercules? I am not a character in a movie or a mythological hero. Names are not important here, I am simply a being of light that serves you all, with love of course.

With the human fixation on time, you would consider me an elder. I have existed for a great period of time you would not yet be able to comprehend.

Have we spoken before?

Yes, many times, in many forms but it was always me, us. The truth is, it was and was not me.

It was my energy in different forms. As all things are the same Source Energy which have taken different forms, so it is with me.

Are you God? I again feel him smile gently.

No.

Is there a God in the way that religion portrays?

No.

Is there a God? A single, omnipotent being who created everything?

Yes.

Do we get to speak with him? Sorry I'm conditioned to think of God as a male energy, a father figure.

There is a Source Energy that you would think of as God but it cannot be explained in simple enough terms even for the most intelligent and gifted minds on earth.

That sounds extremely vague, sorry.

That is unfortunate but it changes nothing. The truth never changes. It just is.

As with your scientific tests, given the same conditions the result will always be the same, no matter who does it or when.

Today, tomorrow or in a thousand years, the same test will produce the same result. As it is with truth, it will always be so.

As quickly as he had drawn close to me, Simon was now gone. Our conversation had come to an end all too soon.

I am somewhat disappointed but I am left feeling grateful for our interaction and comforted to know Spirit will be doing all of the talking. All I have to do is be the transmitter and enjoy the beautiful interactions that will come into my experience and that of those around me.

CHAPTER SIX

Many physical beings

What could I possibly say about this next subject that hasn't been said, filmed, written about or turned into a movie or a video game? Nevertheless I will share my own personal experience with you of the meditations I've had, relating to the many physical beings I believe exist alongside us, evolving with us and assisting us in ways we are yet to fully appreciate or understand.

The following meditation took place on the 3rd November 2018. I set out with the intention of connecting with "aliens" or other highly evolved beings, not only to ask questions but also to be open to receiving any information they desired to share.

I had my own preconceived notions based solely on what I'd seen in movies, documentaries and read in books. My own experience proved to be somewhat different.

Interaction

As a group, you are not ready for open, general communication and interaction. There is too much fear among you. You will reach a stage where it is possible to interact with us harmoniously, but not yet. So in the meantime, we select individuals and small groups of people with which to interact as it is safer for all concerned.

Have you assisted humans who are in positions of power and influence in our society?

Yes, we have allowed some knowledge regarding technology and medical advancement to filter down through various mediums. We have found you to be a beautiful and terrible contradiction of yourselves in the sense that you have used this information to commit horrific atrocities to spread fear and suffering within your group.

However, you have simultaneously eased suffering with new medical techniques, applications of technology and social ad-

vancement. At times you have even enhanced balance with your surroundings and with each other. This is partly the reason why there is not a larger scale interaction between your group and the others who exist around you. We are not so far from your doorstep as you might think.

I have heard people speak of the veil between the spiritual and physical worlds which grows ever thinner during this great awakening we are currently going through.

When these beings told me they are "not so far from your doorstep as you might think" I got the impression it could literally mean they can be in the same room without us even knowing. That is until we are able to attune our vibrational frequency to match theirs and become aware of their presence. It is as if this veil is as thin as the page of a book and seeing them as simple as turning that page.

It was a brief meditation with only a little information received but no matter how in-depth the message or how long I spend in their company, it is always an absolute privilege to be able to interact with them.

I feel honoured and humbled at the same time, not because they act as if superior in any way, which they never do, but because of the energy they have about them. When you are with them they just feel 'evolved'.

When I look at people, society and the state of our world, I am not at all surprised they treat us with caution. They don't fear us but I'm learning that what we do on earth, to each other and the planet itself, has an effect on the rest of the universe, possibly universes and all who exist within it through an unseen connection that I cannot explain. Deep within me I have a knowing that this connection is there, forming a link that can never be broken.

Back in early 2015, whilst this journey of awakening was still all very new to me, I decided to challenge myself to meditate for 30 consecutive days.

I didn't complete the challenge due to a negative energy attaching itself to me and draining me to the point that I looked as though I had aged as well as seeming to be very tired and subdued when I came out of the meditation.

This energy was cleared for me by the head of our psychic circle with a warning to be careful and a reiteration of the fact that we must protect ourselves properly. This is not something about which to be scared it was a lesson learned in knowing how to better interact with the spirit realm without any adverse effects.

Back to the beginning of the challenge, this was the experience I had on day one.

My first time

I am sat on the sofa in the living room of our small apartment. I close my eyes and begin to breathe deeply. As I continue to breathe and gently relax, I gradually feel myself becoming lighter. After a short time, I visualise my soul energy (my higher self you could say) leaving my body but remaining tethered to me by an unseen cord which connects us.

My soul is me, so I will say I from this point.

I see myself leaving the room via the front door and instead of being outside the apartment, I am in a long corridor which slopes gently downward. As I move forward I quickly become aware of a large dark wooden door at the end of the corridor with a brass handle.

I reach out and press downwards on the handle, push the door outwards and step through.

I find myself in a field, I look around and see deep emerald green grass which I feel caressing my bare feet.

Nestled amongst the grass, amazingly beautiful flowers reveal themselves to me. Varieties of red, blue, yellow, purple and orange in full bloom. The sky is clear blue with only the occasional wispy cloud floating by on what is a perfect, warm summer's day.

In the distance, I see a small forest down by a river and feel an urge to go there. I close the large wooden door behind me. The sound of bird song is carried on the gentle breeze sweeping past me as I make my way down.

Closer now, I see a sandy clearing at the edge of the forest that slopes into the river. In the clearing is a lit campfire casting a soft yellow glow on the semi-circle of small tree stumps surrounding it.

I take a seat and gaze out past the fire as the river gently flows toward an unknown destination.

Suddenly I feel a presence. I am not scared but calm, peaceful and accepting of the energy. I see what I would describe as an "alien being" drawing close to me. It feels like a male energy.

He is tall and slim with grey skin and large dark eyes. I sense he is a senior figure of some sort, who also feels very elegant, kind and wise. He begins to speak telepathically to me, communicating that there are many types of aliens throughout the universe.

I feel as if we know each other, have seen each other before and are friends. There are more of his kind drawing close to me now. I am surrounded by them yet I am not afraid. It feels exciting, a real privilege. They look at me and ask,

Do you feel ready?

I answer that I believe so although I am a little nervous of what is to come. They show me pyramids and give me the feeling that they built them or at least assisted.

They are markers for something. I instinctively think of Egypt but am not sure because I also feel there are many more across the world. They go on to say;

We have planted the seed that shall grow into the beautiful flower of friendship.

Suddenly I'm shown the statue of liberty and told;

You will go to America. You shall see us again soon. Be careful with the knowledge that you receive.

This was a short interaction but such a wonderful experience that I truly did not want the meeting to end. I believe these beings are referred to as "the Greys".

They gave me the feeling that they are scientific beings who are also great explorers. For me, they are nothing like the accounts which have previously been given by others who may or may not have had interactions with them. That's not to say these people are wrong, as we each choose the experience we desire to create, it just wasn't my experience.

In my opinion, based on what I have seen so far, it is counterproductive to paint a picture of fear surrounding these beings.

I know that as humans existing in a lower vibrational state we can easily be afraid of what we do not understand but, as I am sure you know, fear does not serve us.

I would suggest we take a more balanced approach. Observe more dispassionately and let go of our ego which is the driving force of fear.

Through meditation, you too may have encounters such as I have had, if you haven't already. This will bring greater understanding and less fear into your experience, which will enable mutual evolution to take place, as well as future large-scale interactions to draw closer for the benefit of us all.

The Greys

The Watchers

Aliens have come through to me in meditation several times since I began this stage of my journey. Generally, I have only felt their energy; their presence.

They have sometimes simultaneously helped me to have a knowing, or an impression, of what they look like, as have the Greys whilst I have been in trance and they were speaking through me. I will discuss trance mediumship in the next chapter.

There have been a couple of occasions at my meeting place, whilst I have been in meditation, when I have seen them standing in front of me.

The image has been so strong that it stayed with me for some time afterwards. I wrote down a description of them which I shared with a friend of Julia and me.

She is an intuitive person and a talented artist who very kindly provided the artwork within this book. Thank you, Ann.

This particular meditation took place on the 15th March 2015.

I am sat at my meeting place, breathing deeply and expanding my energy fields in all directions. I invite beings of divine light and love to draw close to me now. I am ready to communicate.

I feel a presence. I see, with my third eye, several beings drawing close to me. The image is hazy at first but gradually we tune into each other's vibrational frequency and they begin to come into focus.

They're wearing hooded cloaks. The hood is up but does not cover their face. They feel graceful, gentle and calming.

We acknowledge each other and they move closer. I look up toward their faces which are softly rounded with straight, flat noses, small thin mouths and very pointed chins. They had pale blue skin with oval-shaped eyes that had an intense green glow.

Just behind them, I see another figure. A strong male energy. He is a black man with a bald head and very pointed eyebrows. He feels similar to us (as in human) but he is not from Earth. He is wearing a suit and seems to be a senior figure from an organisation of some sort.

He looks directly at me and I sense he wants me to know the words 'Galactic Alliance'. I believe he has facilitated this meeting in some way that I don't yet understand.

I begin to ask questions to the hooded beings. Who are you? Where are you from? What do you want me to know right now?

They graciously answer;

You would call us The Watchers. We oversee your planet and all who exist upon it. We watch over you.

We are teachers of wisdom. We come from beyond the Sun in your solar system. Go to Egypt, visit the pyramids. They are

of great significance. You will know why when you get there.
You will be guided.

Finally, they give me an impression of an American President. They tell me he knows but does not speak out. About what exactly, I cannot be sure as they do not clarify it at that point. As with everything, I imagine all will become clear at the perfect moment, with the perfect outcome for all concerned. They gently drift away.

It was an all-too-brief encounter with only a short message and I am left slightly saddened our meeting has come to an end, for now at least. Yet I feel this was only the beginning of our interactions together.

I could have spent hours in their company. What a blissful awe-inspiring privilege it is, being to able to blend with their energy, to know they are there, watching over us, sharing wisdom gained over many millennia for no other reason than the common purpose of the evolution of all beings.

The Watchers

138

Planet Guardians

After these initial interactions I had become fascinated by what I was experiencing through my meditations and was hungry for more.

Jumping forward to 24th February 2019 I went into meditation with the desire to connect with, for want of a better word, aliens. It had been quite some time since I interacted with any at all so I was grateful to find that a group of beings who were new to me kindly stepped forward to communicate.

Once again I am in my meeting place. I see pale honey-coloured beings of light floating gracefully toward me from above.

There are four of them. I get a sense of femininity about them. They bring my awareness to the light coloured robes they are wearing which go out at the bottom like an A line skirt. I feel as though this is to underline the fact they are feminine energies.

They have long, straight hair and smooth faces with very pointed ears; almost elf like. They look directly at me and I see markings on their faces of three dark blue lines.

There is a short line at the centre of the forehead, from the hair line to the flat, straight nose which looks as if it is a continuation of the marking. This line is flanked by two longer ones which reach down over their narrow oval eyes.

I ask three questions; Who are you? Where are you from? What do you want us to know?

We are Planet Guardians. We take care of many planets throughout the universe, including your own.

We ensure the planet's energy is sustained, balanced and cleansed for as long as it is needed. You are not in control of the destiny of your planet. We are. We enable your planet to be, for as long as you choose to exist upon it.

No matter the action you take, you cannot destroy your planet. It is not permitted. When it is no longer needed it will simply cease to be in its current form. We were created in another dimension that runs parallel to your own but we spend much of our existence moving through multiple dimensions until we fulfill our purpose and return home to rest.

I feel they are about to share something of great significance. One of them suddenly draws close to me, almost nose to nose, as though they are looking deep into my soul. It is as if they are deciding whether or not I am capable of truly comprehending this knowledge.

She leans in ever so slightly as she whispers to me;

8.5 Hz. This frequency is very important, live in balance with Mother Earth for a more peaceful existence. In this way, you will fulfill your purposes both individually and as a group. Do this and witness what you thought to be truth change before your eyes.

This is just a small selection of interactions I have had so far. There have been other meditations where many physical beings stepped forward but I have not always written down what happened and what was shared.

I have simply been caught up in the moment with them, because it is a very uplifting experience due to the positive energy they so generously share with me each time.

This is more of an introduction to a subject which I know will be presented to me in greater detail to be shared in future. I know there are various perspectives about aliens in popular culture and other areas of society.

Many of them are negative but I have heard of positive ones too. In my experience it has been 99% positive with only one negative moment in which an unpleasant negative energy tried to draw close to me in my meeting place.

However, I know that I am in control and with the help of other beings who were present, the energy was quickly pushed away.

It is so important to know how to protect yourself properly and why those of us who are able should be teaching everyone to communicate safely and advance on their journey. I will discuss this a little later in the book.

The truth, as far as I understand it, is that there is an incomprehensible number of beings in existence.

Be it those who reside in our universe and dimension or the many others who exist in the numerous universes and dimensions who have the ability to move through some or all of them.

There are so many interactions to be had but we must evolve together as a group before we can truly know the beings with whom we share our existence.

In the meantime, they wait patiently for us to remember our truth and look on in curious anticipation for the unfolding evolution to occur.

CHAPTER SEVEN

Philosophies, knowledge & guidance

Philosophy can be found everywhere. You only need look with an open heart. What wonders you will see.

Over the course of my journey so far there has been a lot of information to process. It generally falls into three categories for me: philosophy, knowledge and guidance.

Philosophies refers to the wisdom of Source Energy delivered through various physical and spiritual beings. The knowledge comes in the form of many messages about multiple subjects which bring greater understanding for us as a whole and guidance (or advice) for me and others which teaches us what to do with the information we receive, either from the spirit realm or through our own experiences in whichever realm we find ourselves in at that moment.

When I work with Spirit the subjects will vary greatly and can be received in normal meditation or when I go into deep trance and channel one or sometimes multiple beings. They take turns stepping forward and drifting smoothly away again like the ebb and flow of the tide.

There are times when I feel the presence of so many beings wanting to communicate that it can be a little overwhelming. I tell them it's enough for now and ground myself back in this physical realm.

There is still so far for me to evolve and so much for me to learn but the beauty of it is that there is so much to experience too. Every aspect of everything that exists is available to us and I cannot reiterate this point enough.

When you begin to awaken, to become aware of a deeper truth, you will see for yourself the magnificence and beauty of who you are and of all that is.

Know that, from this point on, there is simply no going back.

What follows here is a trance meditation, which was transcribed by Julia one evening as we meditated in the living room.

Monuments and Messages

I breathe deeply and feel myself becoming lighter. Almost immediately I am shown famous landmarks on Earth, the Eiffel Tower, the Statue of Liberty, the Leaning Tower of Pisa and the Great Wall of China. I feel as though they are markers of some sort.

Suddenly I am aware of a powerful presence. We blend our energies, knowing and accepting that we are one. I feel my body expand from within, as though the energy which is my soul instantly swells, and radiates outwards and I am fully connected to the oneness of all things.

The powerful being who has lovingly drawn close begins to speak through me.

Monuments that stand the great test of time. When we reveal ourselves, it is here that we shall appear.

The messenger is coming.

The medium is the messenger. Messages of hope, instruction and practical application. There will be division at first but in the long term there will be unity. Rather than divide and conquer, you will divide and reunite.

Nothing will happen to those who disbelieve, they will simply not receive the tools to be enlightened.

The ones who believe they are in control of your world are not gentle with you but we will be gentle with them.

There are key messages in nature, you only need to look. What wonders you will find.

There is too much separation. You must reunite to become whole again. It will not be easy for you but understand it is simplicity itself. Only you add difficulty to the equation.

Sparks of light are being sent out and various people are receiving messages. You are not the only ones. You will meet (each other) this will be of great benefit to your kind. Seek and you will find... seek and you will find...Eyes are watching curiously in anticipation. What will you do?

There was a long pause here. I feel as if this being had gracefully stepped back to allow another to draw close. I go incredibly cold all over.

Peace be upon you. Quell the fear in your hearts. Embrace the light and love of Source. Enjoy your journey into the after-life.

See, Know, Share.

Accept what is being brought forward as truth. Know it, know yourself, know us. Who are you?...Who are you?... Who are you?

I'm not sure who was asking who this question to be honest. It was as though we were simultaneously asking each other. I was asking with a desire to know or confirm who I instinctively felt was speaking to me and the being was asking with a desire to help me remember who I truly am.

I haven't fully remembered who I am as yet but I can tell you that in the deepest part of me, my instincts were in no doubt as to with whom I was speaking. The one true Source of all that is. I was speaking with God.

I am light. I am love. I am Source. I am the one and the many. I am the all and the nothing. I am everywhere and nowhere, existing in the same moment of now.

I see and yet I have no eyes. I know but do not study. I am and I breathe the breath of life into all things, in all parts of all universes.

All that exists is me and itself.

You may travel far. Further than the countries on your planet. You may know more, simply by being connected to Source. Nothing is hidden. All is shared.

There is much more for you to learn and you will, one step at a time. You only need to choose it. You need not ask. You need only to choose to know what you need to know. Accept that you know it now, whatever it may be.

At this point I hear white noise in my ear. A high pitched tone that signifies I am receiving a new message (a download if you will) from yet another being.

Jesus wants you to know that you are love of the purest form. Aliens do exist and you are on the right path.

There are dark forces in existence yet they are powerless against the light of Source. There are simply many beings of many vibrations providing an experience for the whole.

All things are recorded. This is a truth that you can know beyond all doubt. All is known, all is recorded, all is remembered.

You will start as a ripple in a pond and expand outwards. You will find joy in the design as it is laid out for you. Take pleasure in the plan; in its shape and in its form.

Choose to flow with the unfolding of the experience in a joyful, peaceful way. Do not set rules or laws.

Continue what you are doing and allow yourself to know when to move forward and flow. You will transform like a caterpillar into a butterfly. You will become more aware. Remain more aware.

You will enjoy this.

Conscious Intention

I see a Tibetan Buddhist monk sitting on the floor to my left; legs crossed, deep in thought. He is short in stature and appears to be middle-aged. He looks at me with kind eyes and a knowing smile.

I become aware of another being with a wooden looking face standing in front of me. It could be a mask but I'm not sure. To the right of this being stands an amphibious type of entity.

He is half man, half lizard with dark green scaly skin. He is very large and looks quite intimidating but I feel like he has a soft nature.

He steps forward, leans close to my face and proceeds to gently blow gentle breaths on and around me, almost as if he was bestowing something upon me. I'm not exactly sure of the purpose of this but I do know that I feel humbled by and reverent toward this being.

Sometimes multiple beings will come through in a meditation to help facilitate, strengthen or just simply observe an interaction. With every experience, every interaction, every single thing that occurs throughout the universe, there is always learning to be had, which is, in part, why so many beings draw close to us in meditation.

The monk begins to speak to me in a soft and gentle tone. His voice is soothing and wise;

You create with thought. You manifest with intention.

Learn how to utilise these abilities. Learn to intentionally create your experience and everything that exists within it. Feel the creative energy flowing through your physical being. Know the energy for what it is and harness it. Be gently playful with it and see what you can create.

Everything is possible.

Enjoy the magic of the process. From time to time you will feel yourself expand. This is a signal that you have taken yet another step closer to remembering who you are and fulling your purpose.

Energy is magnetic and like attracts like. Try intentionally attracting what you desire. Observe it, learn from it, move through it and onto the next experience.

Make time to sit and be with Spirit. Allow the words to flow through you and you will be able to share them with others in your realm. It will not always be easy and there will be challenges from which you will learn but it will always be worth it.

Do not worry about anything as there is absolutely nothing to worry about. Be aware and ready yourself now.

Receiving this message left me with the most wonderful feeling of hope; hope for a better future with the knowledge that I don't have to settle for what life throws at me. I don't have to struggle, to live month to month or feel like a victim of circumstance. I am actually the master of my destiny. I am the true creator of my experience.

I am beginning to understand, truly understand, that I am the one who creates and manifests my experiences and I have the power to choose how I observe, receive and learn from all that I encounter.

The Never-Ending Connection

As a flower reaches toward the warmth of the sun, so should the soul reach toward the light of Source. As the flower utilises water to sustain it, so should the soul utilise Source's love in the same way.

For you are the light, the energy if you will, which is born of love. Your light will never die out or relinquish its powerful magnificence. It continues to expand and evolve throughout eternity.

Some say and even believe that when you come to physical realms, particularly lower vibrational denser realms, to experience the physical manifestation of being, you become disconnected from Source Energy, God, Spirit or the Spirits.

You do not.

This connection cannot and will not ever be broken. You will never disconnect from who you truly are. You merely alter your vibrational frequency to align yourself with that which you seek to experience so you may know more and evolve further or, in some cases, to assist those in the process of their evolution who chose you to be a part of their experience before they in-

carnated. So, since you are continuously connected to the oneness that is, we find it interesting that you would still ask; "Why then, do I feel disconnected or feel the need to reconnect with what is?"

You have this feeling because you are experiencing cosmic breathing.

You begin with Source, vibrating at a particular frequency which you then alter so that you may experience all frequencies. This process or journey which you choose to have, is so that you and all that is can devolve, then evolve and complete the expansion and retraction of cosmic breathing.

Once all beings, everything that is made up of the common energy, have completed this journey and returned to Source, it is then that we begin again.

The purpose of this we cannot say for we cannot explain it to you in words which you can comprehend. As we have said to you before, there are no words in many realms, particularly in the higher vibrational and more evolved stages of existence, as there is no need for them.

Communication is done through thought up to the point where there is no need for communication at all. It is a stage of simply being and knowing.

However, the fact remains that you do feel disconnected on this stage of the great journey so, in order to progress, there are ways in which you can return to a more knowingly connected state of being. One of these is remembering to see through your third eye by consciously reopening the pineal gland in your physical brain with this purpose in mind.

You can refer back to how to activate the pineal gland in Chapter Three as well as seek out many different sources of information on how to cleanse, engage and utilise it. Or if you wish you can get in touch with me via any of the contact details at the back of this book to discover more.

Freedom

Take a stand with yourself before you take a stand against others who you feel oppress you in some way. Face yourself in the mirror. Allow it to cause you to reflect upon your true self.

Who are you? What do you believe in? What is your purpose in this life? Who are you?

Sit quietly. Contemplate these questions and gently allow the answers to flow to you. If it feels forced it is your ego speaking. If it flows seamlessly to you then it is us speaking. No, you are not crazy.

You are becoming in tune with your true self and all that is. It will always feel correct to you.

Now let light replace the darkness within. Release the bitterness that so eagerly binds you in self-loathing, anger and hate. You imprison yourself within yourself yet you can be free if you so choose. Freedom is a choice.

It is not given to you by other people. Rather it is given to the self by the self. You may receive guidance with this if you pause long enough to look deep within your consciousness.

Do not hunt down the answers you seek. Learn to let them flow to you as rivers flow to the sea. The flow is constant. You need only remove the barriers placed by you which inhibit what is inevitable.

Stop, sit, breathe and be.

Stop what you are doing right now. Sit comfortably. Breathe deeply in and gently out. Breathe in…and out.

Imagine the clearest, purest white light flowing to you on the slow, relaxed, inward breath. Be aware of the moment between. As you release that breath allow all the negativity, all the darkness and fear that you have held too long inside you to leave you. Feel it leaving you now.

Be in this moment of freedom which is given to you, by you.

Know that through conscious choice, all that you are, all that is, both within and without, is available to you right now. May love drive you and Spirit's light guide you on your path.

Being with Beings

It's Friday afternoon. I'm home early for a change and decide to take the opportunity to meditate with Julia. My intention was to simply go into the quiet, open my chakras, focusing on relaxing and breathing and just to be in the moment. However, it seems Spirit had other plans.

My eyes are closed. After a few deep breaths I begin to relax into my meditation and as I do so I quickly begin to see a man of native American appearance sat in front of me at a small wooden desk.

He is wearing a casual suit but no tie and looks to be around mid-fifties to early sixties in age. He notices me. He knows I am with him. I feel almost as though I am invading his privacy but he isn't at all put out by my presence.

He looks up at me over his thin-rimmed spectacles as if to ask me what I am doing here. I can see that he is writing something and hesitantly asked if he would mind sharing it with me. The expression on his face is focused, thoughtful and slightly serious.

It was a little like how I imagine a university professor would eye up a prospective student or apprentice whilst contemplating if they were up to the task of understanding what they had to offer. He looked away from me to the document on his desk and, as he did so, I felt the first few words come to me like a random thought.

At this point I assumed I would do some automatic writing but Julia had offered to transcribe for me before we started the session so I handed the note pad over to her. I think she knew something I didn't because in the very next moment, I'm deep in trance with the first of several beings who desired to communicate with us.

This native American man was a conduit of Spirit within the spirit realm, relaying to me what had previously come to him. As he shared the words it felt as if he had stepped aside and the being who gave the message to him was now speaking directly to me.

A medium in the spirit realm channelling another Spirit to a medium in the physical realm who was simultaneously channelling the same being to his wife on the sofa. This was a first.

I felt a male energy. He had been an English doctor or psychologist in the physical realm. Now in

Spirit, he had a very powerful presence. I could sense that he was another highly evolved being.

Be humble enough that you would wash the feet of a beggar in the morning though you dine with kings in the evening.

Not for the sake of humility for that is an egocentric thought of the human mind. Rather it is simply to be an aspect of love acting out of love for a fellow being. This is what Source would do.

Truly we say to you that you come from love. You are love itself and you will always be loved.

Shine bright little spark for your light will bring hope to the world. It only takes the smallest spark to illuminate the largest beacon that shares its' light to guide you home. The smallest change in you can have the most profound effect on the whole. Even though you may never see this effect take place, know beyond doubt it is there. It has occurred.

Suddenly I get a big shiver spread throughout my body as I get the familiar cold rush which lets me know another highly evolved being has drawn close, has blended energies with me and is ready to share a message.

I take a deep breath and begin to speak in a deeper more resonant tone of voice than usual. In my soul, at the very core of me, I instinctively feel, as did Julia, that an Angel is here. I feel awestruck and blessed in equal measure as they begin to speak;

The time for games is over. The time to step forward is upon you. Step into the light, bathe in its glory and power. Let it refresh and energise you for what is to come.

Dear soul of souls, you have forgotten much but do not despair, for the moment is coming when you shall remember all that you are.

Faith, knowledge and understanding have their place in the world but more important than this is the ability to allow. Allow yourself to see and do, not just sit and be. Observe your experience, move into it and through it.

Go outside. Do, live, experience and share all that you know; all that you understand and allow others to do with it what they will. This is their choice and their chance to gain faith, knowledge and understanding. Then they too can do, live, experience and share. And so it goes. Do you see?

The flow of the universe is like this.

164

We experience, we observe, we evolve and we repeat this cycle of being until the repetition is no longer needed. Then we return to the source of all things to begin once more this cycle of cosmic breathing.

Now another being steps forward who I feel is a philosopher of an ancient era, possibly Greek or Roman, maybe even Atlantean. I can't be sure. What I do know, feel, is that they are another highly evolved energy.

Again I go cold from head to toe as they draw close and begin to communicate. I ask who is speaking with us.

I am one of many. Many beings, many groups, many worlds, many universes, dimensions and much more. More details will come but not yet. As you are becoming more aware, everything becomes revealed perfectly in the perfect way, at the perfect moment for the highest and best good of all.

When you find yourself lost, when you look around and see no one, when you are full of despair and loneliness, alter your gaze to look within. It is there that we guide you to seek solace, comfort and awareness.

The awareness of hope; the awareness that someone is with you, guiding you.

Offering love, companionship and a simple truth that no matter the experience, no matter the form it takes, you can know deeply that you are never, never, never alone.

You are precious and magnificent beyond words. You are strong. You are gentle. You are light. You are darkness and you are everything in between.

But one thing you absolutely are not, in all the lives you have lived, are living now and will yet live, you are never ever alone.

Our meeting gently comes to an end. The remnants of the interaction with these beings lingers with me for a moment as I give thanks for this blessed experience.

I breathe deeply, close down my chakras and ground myself in the physical plain once more. I know that whatever path these coming years take me on, whatever experiences are to be had, whatever lessons are to be learned, I will not do it alone.

For as much as I exist in a physical world and obviously have my family and friends with me, I know that on a deeper level I have access to all I will ever need to assist me on this journey. A journey I chose to see out to its conclusion all those years ago as a child in East London, and for this, I am truly grateful.

It All Begins With Breathing

Meditation leads to transformation. Transformation leads to awareness. Awareness leads to understanding and understanding leads to the evolution of us all.

These have been my meditations which it has been my pleasure and privilege to share with you. My hope now is that is has sparked a desire within you to begin meditating also. If it has and you're wondering how to get started, here is a basic introduction you can follow and practice until you are ready for whatever comes next.

Breath first and the rest will follow.

My first meditative experience was to sit quietly in a relaxing environment where I could be alone and undisturbed. I would close my eyes and focus on taking deep, slow, relaxed breaths until I felt that I had relieved the stress or anger I was trying to manage.

This is a simple but effective place to start as, even when you delve deeper into meditation and you find your mind wandering, it is the constant that can re-centre you so you may focus more clearly.

Find somewhere you too can be alone and undisturbed. Take five, ten or even fifteen minutes to sit quietly and take deep slow relaxed breaths whilst you draw your attention to the feeling of the breath going in through your nose and out again.

Close your eyes. Feel the gentle rise and fall of your chest as you continue to breathe and gradually let go of any tension in your face, neck, shoulders, arms, hands, legs and feet. Feel the tension leaving you with each breath.

Feel each care, worry and stress leave you. Simply continue to breathe in this way until you feel completely relaxed in this moment of now.

Begin to visualise in your mind as you breathe in through your nose, that you are drawing a pure, clear, white light into your mind and body. Feel it entering and flowing throughout the entirety of your being and, as you breathe out, release the darkness which has weighed you down, stressed you out and negatively affected your experience.

Continue with this breathing and visualisation until you feel lighter than you did when you began.

When you are ready, open your eyes and simply be in this new moment of now with a renewed sense of peace, positivity and possibility as you move forward on your journey.

Practice this simple technique as often as you can, remembering to focus on your breathing. Let go of all that you need to and allow the benefit of it to take place within you.

This is enough to get you started in meditation but, of course there will be so much more for you to discover along this path of enlightenment and you will, in the perfect way, at the perfect moment, for the perfect outcome. As it is with all things.

A final thought

I am the kind of person who never thought they could write an essay without extreme difficulty let alone a book of any kind, yet here we are at the end.

The meditative process of creating this book with Spirit, along with the fact it is now ready to be shared, has been an incredible journey for me personally. It has given me a renewed focus and a deeper connection with the oneness that is.

It has shown me that I can be more than I was taught to be, more than I thought I could be and more than I was always afraid to be and has brought a deeply powerful healing to me.

I understand now that I am worthy of all that is good and of all the wonderful possibilities which lay ahead.

As much as this book has affected me in a positive way already and will continue to do so, I wonder more how it has affected you.

At the end of each meditation I could have explained in detail my thoughts or perspectives but I know what I think and feel about it already, so I decided not to in the hope it will encourage you to contemplate what you think and feel about it.

You can find details of how to contact me at the end of the book if you wish to share your own thoughts and experiences on what is shared here.

I know that my main purpose in this life is to receive and share information and this book is a major step along my path of evolution. However, just as important as my evolution is yours, for the more you evolve the more we all do.

If you have questions I invite you to receive the answers. If you are wounded in some way I invite you to receive healing. If there are dark places within I invite you to receive the light of Spirit so that you may illuminate what was hidden.

Observe what it brings you and gently release it to the universe, letting go of the experience once and for all; finally allowing the void which is created by this process to be filled with a higher vibrational aspect of experience.

Allow yourself to feel the freedom which is yours then help others to know the same freedom which is theirs, by sharing all that you have learned and all that you have remembered.

Observe the magnificent beauty of Source Energy enabling the evolution of us all through your experiences, your knowledge, your understanding and above all else your love, our love, the one love of the one consciousness that exists in harmony with all that is.

May your journey be blessed with an abundance of experience, so we all may evolve and return once more to that from which we came:

Home. Love. Source.

Further Information

I would like to thank you for taking the time to read this book and hope it has touched your life in a positive way.

If you have any questions or would like to share your thoughts and experiences I would love to hear from you. This is a great way for me to receive feedback and will help me to be able to share and inspire people further.

You comments and reviews are always appreciated. If you wish you can do this on amazon or my facebook page.

Lastly, if you would like to follow me on social media or even just have a conversation on any related subject area you may do this via any of the contact details listed. I very much look forward to hearing from you in future.

Contact details

Gmail: mybeingwithbeings@gmail.com

Facebook: Being in conversation

Instagram: @beingwithbeings

Twitter: @beingwithbeings

Printed in Poland
by Amazon Fulfillment
Poland Sp. z o.o., Wrocław